A HUNDRED
CAMELS

A HUNDRED CAMELS

A Mission Doctor's Sojourn and Murder Trial in Somalia

Gerald L. Miller
with Shari Miller Wagner

Foreword by
Shirley Hershey Showalter

DreamSeeker Books
TELFORD, PENNSYLVANIA

an imprint of
Cascadia Publishing House

Copublished with
Herald Press
Scottdale, Pennsylvania

Cascadia Publishing House orders, information, reprint permissions:
contact@CascadiaPublishingHouse.com
1-215-723-9125
126 Klingerman Road, Telford PA 18969
www.CascadiaPublishingHouse.com

A Hundred Camels
Copyright © 2009 by Cascadia Publishing House LLC
Telford, PA 18969
All rights reserved
DreamSeeker Books is an imprint of Cascadia Publishing House LLC
Copublished with Herald Press, Scottdale, PA
Library of Congress Catalog Number: 2009006936
ISBN 13: 978-1-931038-54-6; ISBN 10: 1-931038-54-6
Book design by Cascadia Publishing House
Cover design by Dawn Ranck; cover art and interior camel
drawings by Vienna Wagner, copyright © 2009

The paper used in this publication is recycled and meets the
minimum requirements of American National Standard for Information Sciences—
Permanence of Paper for Printed Library Materials, ANSI Z39.48-1984.1984

Library of Congress Cataloguing-in-Publication Data
Library of Congress Cataloging-in-Publication Data

Miller, Gerald L., 1937-
A hundred camels : a mission doctor's sojourn and murder trial in Somalia /
Gerald L. Miller with Shari Miller Wagner ; foreword by Shirley Hershey
Showalter.
   p. cm.
ISBN-13: 978-1-931038-54-6 (pbk. : alk. paper)
ISBN-10: 1-931038-54-6 (pbk. : alk. paper)
1. Miller, Gerald, 1937- 2. Missionaries, Medical--Somalia--Biography. 3. Trials (Murder)--Somalia. 4. Mennonites)--Somalia. I. Wagner, Shari, 1958- II.
Title.
R722.32.M555 2009
610.92--dc22
   [B]

                    2009006936

16 15 14 13 12 11 10 09   10 9 8 7 6 5 4 3 2

To Mary, my partner of over fifty years,
who went with me to Somalia despite her misgivings:
You remain the love of my life.

To Shari, Marlis, and Stephen,
who shared the year with us in East Africa:
I am so proud of each of you.

To Shea, Kyle, Vienna, Alexander, and Iona,
my beloved grandchildren:
May you find strength in your own journeys.

CONTENTS

FOREWORD:
THE ONE HUNDREDTH
NAME FOR GOD

This book contains an equal measure of travelogue, mystery story, medical diary, and cultural history. Underneath the excitement of the courtroom drama, murder trial, and many escapades in a new culture lies the story of how one man's spirit grew, first in his own country and his own faith and then in a new country with a different faith. Welcome to spiritual autobiography as only a Mennonite medical missionary could write it.

The number *100* plays a significant role in Dr. Miller's story because it is an important number in both Muslim religion and Somali culture. A crucial piece of information, explaining the title, is that the blood price for a murdered male in this culture in 1972 was one hundred camels.

But the number 100 plays another, more subtle role. Somali prayer necklaces contain 33 beads that are fingered three times each during which time the 99 names of Allah are uttered. One name for Allah exists, not in the mind of human beings but in the mind of another creature, a nearly sacred animal in Somalia—the camel. The camel contemplates what humans cannot know—the one hundredth, unmentionable, name for God.

Throughout this book the careful reader can find many clues about the mysterious nature of God as the young, humble, resourceful Midwestern American doctor attempts to share his faith in action. Curiosity is one of his gifts. Even though he has an incredible number of medical and language challenges, he does not focus just on work. In his youth Dr. Miller thought he would become a veterinarian. He grew up on a small farm and continues to be fascinated by animals. Africa opened great opportunities to explore the animal kingdom, and he shares this amazing world with the reader. He is alert to the signs of the holy, connecting all of nature to its Creator, and recognizes the central role of the resilient desert animal, the camel.

Because Dr. Miller deeply respects the Muslim culture in which he finds himself as an emergency replacement on a one-year assignment, he does not question either the 99 names for God or the unknown hundredth one. Having asked God at the very beginning of the time in Somalia for help "that we might show through our actions Jesus' love," Dr. Miller's prayer is answered. He sees God in other people.

These people have names like Martha, Pauline, Elsie, Chester, Catherine, Harold, Barbara, Neil, Margaret, Velma, Anna, Mary, Shari, Marlis, Stephen, Perry, and Lucille. They also have names such as Hussein Sadad Hassan, Fatuma Abdulle Mohamed, Hassen Nur, Mariam Mohammed Hassen, Lul Abdurahman Hussein, Mohamed Aden, Omar, Ibrahim, Uglo, Akim, Hawa, Lul, and Abdi.

He sees God in the Southern Cross constellation in the night sky and goes to sleep to the "circular beat" of drums. He sees God in the "bright orange flowers of the flamboyant trees" and the "fragrance of white frangipani blossoms." He sees God in all the presenting problems of his patients—cataracts (he teaches himself how to do surgeries and provides sight to scores of people), worms, wounds, rabies, leprosy. If the patient needs his rare blood type, he gives his own. If a baby loses his mother in childbirth, he brings the child into his own home. He recognizes the wisdom in the ancient proverbs he hears and incorporates many more into the written version of his story more than thirty years later.

Because he looks for God, finding new names for God in a Muslim, African, country, Dr. Miller is prepared to pass his greatest test: trial for murder. What is most amazing to me about this story is not how big a role it played in his life—but how small. When one lives within a community in which Jesus and his willingness to suffer for the sake of love is one's true north—or Southern Cross—false accusations with potential felony, or even capital, consequences lose their ability to shake the ground upon which one walks.

Dr. Miller tells us that a chance encounter on an airplane prompted him to think about writing his story. We can imagine that an unmentionable name for God passed between these two men sitting side-by-side. And we can imagine a camel lumbering along in Jamama, Somalia, smiling.

—Shirley H. Showalter, Vice-President—Programs at the Fetzer Institute, Kalamazoo, Michigan; and former President, Goshen College, can be reached at www.100memoirs.com.

AUTHOR'S PREFACE

Over the decades, I've told only a few people the full story of my year in Somalia. I've given many Somali slide shows in which I describe treating tuberculosis and snakebites, but I've rarely spoken of my murder trial. Until last year, when she started reading the manuscript of this book, even my own sister didn't know about the trial. My reticence to talk about this experience has not been because I've wanted to keep it a secret—but because the story is so complicated; it takes so much explanation to convey an understanding of the events so that they can be seen in their context.

A few years ago, while flying for about four hours between San Francisco and Chicago, I struck up a conversation with a businessman. As we discussed our international travels, I brought up my experiences in Somalia, and he started asking questions. He took such a keen interest that I found myself going into great detail about my year in Somalia and telling him the whole account of my trial. Before we disembarked in Chicago, this businessman told me that my story had given him a different view of missionaries and of service in a Muslim country. He encouraged me to tell the story to others.

Ecclesiastes, chapter three, asserts that "for everything there is a season . . . a time to keep silence and a time to speak." A Somali proverb also speaks of the cyclic nature of time: "If you live long you will see how the camels are born." I couldn't have written this memoir on our return from Somalia in 1972; some of the material was too sensitive. The Revolutionary government was still in power, and mission workers were still in the country. Then, too, my wife and I were busy being members of the Markle community and raising our family. Now, with my retirement from medical practice and my daughter Shari's willingness to help me craft this book, it seemed like an appropriate season to reflect upon what was the most momentous year of my life.

A Hundred Camels, though, is not just my story. It is part of the story of the Mennonite Mission in Somalia and of the Somalis who became my friends. In fact, the hero of this book, the one who turns the tragic caravan of events, is a Somali. My hope is that these chapters speak in a way that deepens cultural understanding and concern for the current crisis in Somalia where continual violence has created more than one million refugees.

Though the events in this book are now decades old, they take place in a culture where values and beliefs change very slowly. Part of this story is an ageless one: how good blossoms from corruption, how integrity knows no ethnic boundaries, how one moral stand makes a difference.

—*Gerald L. Miller, M.D.*
Westfield, Indiana

ACKNOWLEDGMENTS

From the Author

I would like to express, first of all, my deep appreciation to Shari, my daughter, who took time from her own writing projects to help me compose this memoir. My first drafts tended to focus on the facts, but she constantly prodded me to probe deeper into my feelings, to describe settings and create dialogue. She organized the flow of the chapters and strengthened my prose. Because Shari was an eighth grader during our year in Somalia, she already had some understanding of the culture and knew about many of the events in this book. *A Hundred Camels* would not have been written without her constant encouragement and her professional editorial skills.

I want to acknowledge my wife's assistance, too, in writing this book. Mary and I have spent many pleasant hours reminiscing about our year in Somalia. In recalling events, it helped greatly that Mary had faithfully written weekly letters to her parents, John and Ruth Mishler, and to her sister, Doris Mast, and that they had returned this correspondence to us. Our close friends in Markle, Don and Marlene Hoopingarner and Jerry and Jean Mossburg, also saved our letters and gave them to us as I began writing. Without these letters, as well as the ones we sent to Shari and her sister Marlis while they attended a Kenyan boarding school, Mary and I might still be arguing over some of the details that happened those many decades ago.

Furthermore, I want to convey my appreciation to the Markle Medical Center. This organization made our year in Somalia possible by providing financial, emotional, and spiritual support. The Center also saved correspondence from which I extracted memories of patients I treated in the Jamama clinic.

Finally, I would like to recognize the dedicated mission personnel I describe in these chapters, both American and Somali. They were our true mentors and supporters as the mission was a team effort. During our year, we greatly valued support from the Eastern Mennonite Board of Missions and Charities. This organization has long had a heart for the Somali people and a profound understanding of how to work amid cultural differences.

I've written this book as I experienced Somalia in my thirty-fourth year, as someone who had lived all of his life in Indiana without any specific preparation for understanding Somali culture. Certainly, some incidents might be understood differently by the more seasoned missionary and, especially, by a Somali. I would ask for forgiveness whenever that is the case.

—*Gerald Miller, M.D.*

From the Editor

The Somali proverb, "One finger cannot wash a face," comes to mind as I consider all the people who have contributed to the effort of preparing *A Hundred Camels* for publication.

First of all, my gratitude goes to my my daughter, Vienna, who created the Sufi-inspired mandala on the book cover, and to my husband, Chuck, a fellow poet and English teacher, who spent the first part of a summer vacation examining these chapters and suggesting changes. Thanks also goes to my friend, Elizabeth Weber, a poet and professor at the University of Indianapolis, who graciously read *A Hundred Camels* and offered her perceptive feedback. Bertha Beachy and Ivan Leaman, M.D., former long-term mission workers in Jamama, Somalia, scrutinized the manuscript for cultural and historical accuracy and members of my writers breakfast group—Ryan Ahlgrim, Rod Deaton, J. Daniel Hess, and Martha Yoder Maust, M.D.—read it from a literary perspective. My friends Felix and Ada Canal increased my understanding of my father's trial by translating Italian court records into English while Asli Aden Ashker, a former nursing student from Jamama, patiently answered our questions about her memories of the mission hospital and about what has happened to the Somalis we once knew. To all of these people, my heartfelt thanks for your generous sharing of time and expertise.

I also want to acknowledge publications that were important in the crafting of *A Hundred Camels*. Many of the Somali proverbs come from G. L. Kapchits' book, *To Know Something for Sure, One Would Even Part with a She-Camel: Somali Proverbs, A Study in Popularity* (The Way, Moscow, 2002). Other valuable sources include Omar Eby's book, *Fifty Years, Fifty Stories: The Mennonite Mission in Somalia, 1953-2003* (DreamSeeker Books of Cascadia Publishing House, Telford, Pa., 2003) and I. M. Lewis' *The Modern History of Somaliland* (Weidenfeld and Nicolson, London, 1965) and *Understanding Somalia: Guide to Culture, History and Social Institutions* (HAAN Associates, London, 1993).

—*Shari Miller Wagner*

Somalis can lie,
but their lie will never become a proverb.
—Somali Proverb

PROLOGUE

At eight in the morning the air already felt still and heavy as I shifted my weight on a shaky bench adjacent to the south wall of the courtroom. Somalis from the Kismayu region, seated on boards placed over cement blocks, packed the large room. Onlookers, pressed three deep, peered through the open windows.

The white-washed walls stood bare except for a photograph of General Mohamed Siad Barre, the president of Somalia, dressed in a stiff military uniform. When the judge in a long, black gown entered the room two and a half hours later, all rose to their feet until he sat down at a table beneath the general's stolid gaze.

I was the American doctor from the Jamama Mennonite Hospital, and I was being accused of the murder of Hussein Sadad Hassan. It seemed like a long time before the judge spoke. He kept thumbing through his thick stack of papers, which did nothing to alleviate my anxiety. Finally, he read in Somali the accusation against me and his words were translated into English. "How do you plead—guilty or not guilty?" he asked.

I answered in English, "Not guilty."

Murmurs in Somali coursed through the crowd as the judge translated my response into Arabic for the court reporter. This was the start of my long day in court.

PART ONE

"He who has not traveled in
the world has no eyes."

—*Somali Proverb*

CHAPTER ONE

You should expect from people and the forest
what one cannot predict.
—Somali Proverb

The event that led to my trial, the court case of the decade for the district of southern Somalia, occurred on August 25, 1971, the night before I arrived in the country. I had traveled from the small town of Markle, Indiana, to serve a one year assignment as the only doctor at the Jamama Hospital. When my wife, Mary, my four-year-old son, Stephen, and I stepped off the East African Airways plane and into the stifling heat of Mogadishu's runway, we were entering the Horn of Africa, an area known in earlier centuries as the Sesame Land or the Land of Punt. I worried that we would not recognize our escort, since we had never met any of the Somali mission personnel, but after going through customs and coming out in the baggage area, I realized that the only other white man at the airport was Harold Reed, the administrator of the Somalia Mennonite Mission.

As Harold drove us through narrow streets, he proved adept at dodging the donkeys, carts, lorries, cars, and people who swarmed everywhere. Watching him maneuver around a man pushing a wheel barrow piled high with sacks of cement, I wondered if I'd ever feel comfortable enough to drive through those crowded, chaotic streets. Many Somalis carried bundles on their backs, and on their heads the women also balanced large baskets bulging with such market items as mangoes and eggplants. Mixed in with these busy laborers and shoppers were younger, more affluent men who wore suits and sported brief cases. Harold said these were the new professional and government workers.

The buildings we drove past were mostly white cement with flat roofs, but one edifice under construction was more colorful and larger than the rest. It appeared to be almost completed.

"That's a theater for the arts the Chinese are building and giving to the city," Harold told us. "Right now, China is giving a lot of aid to Somalia, but the Chinese who have moved here try to keep a low profile. They live in areas of the city by themselves."

I started noticing, then, the Chinese, who were much shorter than the average Somali, walking briskly along the sidewalks.

Finally we arrived at the mission, a compound enclosed by white block walls with broken bottle glass cemented to their top ridges. A watchman opened the gate to let our vehicle enter. The Reeds' house and the guest house stood directly on our right, and several houses for single personnel were on our left. As we climbed a hill, we also passed the home of Neil and Margaret Reimer. Neil, a Canadian, taught business classes and served as business manager for the Somali mission. During the course of the year, he became my chess partner and we always had a game underway whenever I passed through the city.

At the top of the hill spread the largest building on the compound, a one-story school for adult evening classes. Many students stood milling nearby. Although they all seemed friendly, offering at least a few words of English greeting as we got out of the car, the walled compound, the jagged glass, the guarded gate, and the armed soldiers on the street still made me uneasy.

Later that evening, as a red sun loomed above the skyline of government buildings, the night watchman let loose two large dogs to roam the compound for the night.

"These dogs do more for our protection than anything else we could do to protect ourselves," Harold told me.

"But how will we be able to move between houses?" I asked.

"They know who should be in and who shouldn't," he answered. "And because you are white, they will never bother you."

I can vividly recall that first evening, since I was reeling from culture shock and feeling sad about saying good bye to our daughters, Shari and Marlis, earlier that day at the Nairobi airport. As there was no possibility for them to attend school in Somalia, they would be boarding at Rosslyn Academy, a Mennonite-administered school situated on an old British coffee plantation outside of Nairobi. My parents, who had traveled with us, were just beginning a three-year assignment to teach at Rosslyn, so at least we felt better knowing that our daughters would have grandparents nearby.

As Mary, Stephen, and I sat with the Reeds around their table that evening for a meal of goat, eggplant with cheese casserole, and fresh mangoes, we learned that Somalia was the second-poorest country in the world behind Upper Volta. The government, led by General Mohamed Siad Barre, President of the Supreme Revolutionary Council of the Somali Democratic Republic, was approaching its second anniversary. We had seen its soldiers with machine guns posted at the airport and striding through the streets. We learned that this new regime was trying to bring peace and order to a region troubled by long-standing tribal violence and governmental corruption.

After our meal, while Stephen ran off to climb a mango tree with the youngest Reed daughter, Harold and his wife, Barbara, described some of the dangers which might become a possibility during the year. We had heard of Merlin Grove's death, nine years earlier at this same mission compound, and we had read the book, *A Whisper in a Dry Land,* by Omar Eby, which told the story of a radical young mullah who came into the compound and stabbed Merlin in the chest. The clerical robe he wore that evening concealed a dagger while he waited with parents registering students for the Mahaday Primary School. Suddenly, the mullah jumped forward, killing Merlin in an attempt to purge his country of the *gaals* or infidels. The man also stabbed Merlin's wife, Dorothy, three times in the abdomen as she was running up the hill toward the turmoil, but she survived the attack. We also knew of the incident that occurred in 1959 on this same compound, when Rhoda Lind, a teacher and homemaker, was slashed about the face and hands by a night-time intruder in her home. But we had only heard of these incidents after accepting our assignment.

That evening Harold outlined on a map what our escape routes would be from different places in Somalia if for some reason we needed to leave the country immediately. I was most concerned about what the emergency route would be from our base in Jamama.

Harold told us that we would head from our village to the Indian Ocean. To reach the ocean by motor vehicle meant a thirty-mile trip to Kismayo, which was the way we would normally go to the beach while we lived in Jamama.

"But if you need to flee quickly," Harold said, "go straight across the desert and bush country, preferably at night. This is a distance of only four or five miles. There are no roads leading straight to the ocean. You will need to walk and take nothing with you but enough water and food for a couple of days. Wear clothing that will protect you from the thorn bushes and sun and good shoes to protect your feet. Once you're at the beach, you'll watch for a boat that will pick you up. It will most likely come from the south, from Kenya."

Harold reiterated that he did not expect us to need an

emergency escape route. Still, because of anti-American attitudes in the government and our status as mission workers in a Muslim country, we should always have a plan.

That night Mary and I prayed for the safety of our family and the mission workers as well as for God's help in reaching the Somalis with compassionate medical care. We prayed that we might show through our actions Jesus' love.

We fell asleep unaware that, the night before, a speeding Toyota had swerved on the road between Kismayu and Jamama. Two hundred and eighty miles from Mogadishu, the car overturned with two men and two women inside. The thirty-year-old driver had been drinking, a practice forbidden by Muslim law, but the driver, as often happens, was not injured. The two women in the back seat had moderate injuries; those of the gentleman in the front passenger seat were more severe.

The wounded were brought in a truck bed to Jamama Hospital and given emergency treatment by the nurses. Then they waited four days for the new doctor's arrival.

CHAPTER TWO

A brother is like one's shoulder.
—Somali Proverb

On our second day in Somalia, a Friday, the Islamic Holy Day, Harold suggested that all the mission staff go to the beach for breakfast and fellowship. As we drove through the downtown, I noticed its emptiness compared to the previous workday. We passed by many beautiful buildings, including the gleaming, white mosque of the sacred Sheikh Abdulaziz with its stately minaret. I had read that this mosque is twelve hundred years old, but oral tradition says it was never built but rose on its own. I found it remarkable that the Sheikh Abdulaziz was still in good condition. What building from my home state of Indiana was even two hundred years old?

Mogadishu faced the Indian Ocean, but, unlike a waterfront in U.S. cities, there were no large hotels or beach houses. On foot, we climbed small sand dunes to approach the white, empty beach. Waves rose a couple of feet before crashing on the sand, but, farther out, the water was a deep, placid blue as far as our gaze would take us. A mild breeze blew off the ocean from the east. Stephen and I removed our sandals and waded in the ocean's warmth.

Soon our new friends opened their baskets and began spreading out homemade bread, cheese, and fresh fruits. The men built a fire, but just as we started frying the eggs, the wind picked up, making it hard to keep flames going. Blankets wouldn't stay on the ground, and the eggs were salted with sand. Our cheese and bread also had a grainy coating, and, as the wind increased, it blew sand into our mouth and eyes. I understood why Somalis weren't spending their day of rest at the beach. We had devotions, then headed back to the compound just as the sun became unbearably hot and its glint off the water made it hard to look at the ocean.

On Saturday, Harold and I drove north of Mogadishu to the mission school at Jowhar and the health clinic and maternity ward at Mahaday. We took the Land Rover over a road Mussolini built in the early 1930s. The first section of the road, which took us to Jowhar, sixty miles away, had been resurfaced rather recently, but the further from Jowhar we drove, the rougher the road grew, so that the twenty miles to Mahaday took at least two hours.

When Mussolini's road was first built, the Italians erected large cement markers every ten kilometers with the distance written in Roman numerals. The markers were about four feet high, three feet wide, and eight inches thick. But a number of the holes in the road were bigger than these signs, so it was impossible to skirt all of the chasms. Some you had to drop down into and then hope you could muster enough power to emerge.

This trip also introduced me to military police checkpoints. Harold could pass through them with ease, since the police already knew him from other trips. But they were interested in who I was and where I was going. Harold, speaking fluent Somali, introduced me as a new doctor and explained that we were carrying supplies to Mahaday. The police searched the boxes rapidly, and we were on our way.

The two American nurses at the clinic, Velma Eshleman and Anna Lutz, were seasoned mission workers who knew the Somali language well and had served in developing world medical clinics for a number of years. They appeared extremely busy. For three days each week, they saw many children, pregnant women, and adults with both acute and chronic illnesses. Other days they handled emergencies and made house calls or public health visits. In an old building renovated into a maternity ward, they performed uncomplicated deliveries and kept mothers a day or two to get the newborns off to a healthy start.

The tall, wooden shelves on one wall of the dispensary were well-stocked with vaccines, vitamins, aspirin, and chloroquine tablets. On the bottom shelf, three large brown bottles held different liquids: one contained de-worming medicine; another, diarrhea medicine for children; and a third, cough medicine. I recognized a small bottle of sulfa liquid and a bottle of penicillin tablets but noticed that the clinic needed more medicines for tropical diseases. The nurses also mentioned that they were short of medicines for chronic diseases such as hypertension, arthritis, and tuberculosis.

Anna and Velma wanted my advice, particularly on how to treat such chronic medical problems as asthma, hypertension, diarrhea, and arthritis. "We're using a ten- year-old protocol leaflet for our treatment of parasitical diseases and the usual acute illnesses," Anna explained. "We badly need an updated treatment schedule. Some of the medicines on our list we can't even buy." She went on to ask where they could get the medicines at the best prices and if I could get them medicines in bulk from Kenya when I ordered them for the Jamama hospital.

After visiting the clinic and maternity ward, we sat around Anna and Velma's kitchen table while they handed me charts of patients about whom they had questions. Suddenly I felt overwhelmed. They asked me to supply information on tropical diseases I had only read about. Without any knowledge of the services available from hospitals, pharmacies, and the government, I had no idea how much money I would have to purchase medicines and supplies.

I could stay busy full-time just at Mahaday, but I had not even arrived at my greatest responsibility—Jamama Hospital. I knew I'd need to learn my duties quickly since a lot of people were depending on me. But even then, I underestimated the extent to which doctors were needed in Somalia. I learned later that in 1971 there were only 156 medical doctors in the whole country. Seventy were Somali; the rest—except for me and one part-time Canadian doctor—were Russian, Chinese, or with UNICEF. If all the doctors were practicing, that meant one doctor for every 22,000 people. But these doctors weren't evenly distributed; most worked in the four largest cities.

Before I left that afternoon, I promised Anna and Velma I would update their protocol sheets, correspond with them about medicines, and be back to visit in several weeks when I could stay longer. I was impressed by what these two dedicated nurses were providing with no supporting services and such meager supplies.

The next day was a Sunday, and Mogadishu's late morning streets teemed with carts, cars, and people as Harold drove us to the airport. With the windows rolled down, I breathed in the sharp scent of charcoal smoke mixed with incense and musk. Once, in the market district, when our vehicle halted amid the congestion of pedestrians, a young man reached in the back window to grab Mary's purse. Fortunately, she had a firm grip on it and the assailant fled empty-handed.

When we finally boarded our aircraft, an old 1940s military propeller plane, we were stunned to discover that most of the seats had been removed. Boxes of cargo were stacked in the back, and two soldiers with machine guns sat behind us. The entry door in the middle of the plane did not close tightly, so I could see the desert below for the whole rough and noisy ride. We found it difficult to balance trays with orange Fantas on our laps, and we had to think of ways to entertain Stephen so that he wouldn't stare at the soldiers. Although the flight felt as bumpy as a rickety amusement park ride, we had been told it was faster and more comfortable than taking the thirteen-hour bus trip.

Forty minutes later, we landed on a sod airstrip at the edge of Kismayu. Chester Kurtz, our Jamama administrator, walked up to meet us. A tall, thin gentleman with a keen sense of humor, he greeted me with, "So you are my new tennis partner," and I could envision that, with his long arms and legs, I was in for a challenge.

Chester was principal of the school and also taught the science courses. He did all this, plus he was in charge of maintenance for the compound. Chester had been in Somalia from 1955 to '59 as one of the first mission workers and had been involved in agricultural projects with the Somalis. After he married his wife, Catherine, they returned together in 1962 and had been at Jamama for the prior nine years.

We traversed the first twenty miles on fairly nice blacktop with only a few potholes, but the last ten miles turned into a dirt road with no base and many ruts and large holes that had to be navigated at a slow speed. Crossing zero latitude, we spotted the twenty-foot-high cement marker that signified the equator. We pulled over once to watch baboons romping at the shady base of a baobab tree, and we also stopped for a military checkpoint.

Chester indicated to the police that I was the new doctor for Jamama and that this was my family. They looked through some of our suitcases, and I remember one officer pulling out my rechargeable Norelco shaver and wanting to know what kind of camera it was. He had difficulty understanding how I could shave with it. He knew we weren't bringing any forbidden guns but was curious about our odd belongings.

The land appeared desolate, with few trees and only scrawny, brown bushes. This was the dry season, and everything was exceedingly parched. It was also windy, and at times we saw dust clouds scurrying along the ground. We passed a few small villages, but Mary and I were so excited about our arrival at the mission compound that we did not really assimilate all these strange sights.

When we reached Jamama, we caught a glimpse of its downtown: several cement houses with tin roofs and small stores that banked the dirt street. We passed a post office and a police station, both flying the Somali flag—a white, five-pointed star on a background of sky blue—then we turned off the road and drove through the mission compound's open gate.

On our right, some young Somali men and women stood in front of the faded green hospital. When they saw us, they smiled and waved, apparently eager to catch a glimpse of the new doctor and his family. I was also looking forward to meeting each of them. A couple hundred feet further on the left were the tan school buildings. Then, at the end of the drive, behind a dirt tennis court on the left and a basketball court on the right, stood four small, cement houses.

Chester pointed to a house on the far right that was the same faded green as the hospital. "That's your house, and everything is ready for you." He didn't have time to say more because, as we stepped out of the Fiat, we were met by mission personnel coming from all directions. After rather hurried greetings, Catherine Kurtz, a lean, kind-faced woman, invited us all into her home for some orange Fantas, a welcome gesture after such a hot, dusty ride. We realized that Catherine had a gift for hospitality as she asked questions and listened intently to our answers. She knew what information we needed to put us at ease, and we could feel her immediate acceptance. I could tell she and Mary would get along well during the year.

Chester and Catherine's two oldest children, Marianne and Jewel, were already at Rosslyn where our daughter, Marlis, a fourth-grader, would room with Marianne. Their other two children were boys—Eric, a year older than our Stephen and Eugene, two years younger. Stephen was soon outside with Eric, herding the compound's goats and getting acquainted with the two day-guards.

I had been looking forward to meeting the two American nurses who would be working with me in the hospital, clinic, and nursing school. One of them, Martha Horst, a fair-skinned Wisler Mennonite from Ohio, greeted me with, "It's about time you got here. We are tired of carrying the load, and now we can take a vacation and leave you." Fortunately, she was only joking. I asked Martha what she did in the hospital.

"I've been in Jamama now for two years," she explained, "and I'm starting my third. I work mostly in the clinic, seeing patients in the mornings and supervising the hospital employees. I make sure that we have supplies and that everyone is doing their job. I also help with the public health program, and Pauline and I trade call every other night at the hospital for questions from the night nurses and for obstetrical deliveries."

I told her I was impressed and hoped to help her with that responsibility. Some people just have good insight and judgment, and I sensed immediately and accurately that Martha had both of these traits, as well as sound medical knowledge and the confidence necessary to lead others in their tasks.

Pauline Zimmerman, the other nurse, was from Pennsylvania and had been in Somalia for only one year but was learning the language quickly. The other mission workers said she had to learn the Somali word for "no," *bis,* soon after her arrival. She was frequently presented with gifts from young men who would ask if she would marry them. She was young and a little overweight, which made her very attractive to these men, some of whom might also have been looking for a ticket to the States. I would be working with Pauline in the nursing school. Although she organized all of the classes and performed most of the instruction, she told me that I would be teaching some of the medical courses. She would supervise the second-year students in the hospital and take hospital and delivery call every other night. I knew I would need to be in charge of the hospital, clinic, and nursing school, at least in name, but I could tell from that first conversation that this would be a team effort.

I was also introduced to Elsie Cressman, a midwife who had worked in East Africa for a number of years but for the past two months had been in Jamama, helping to deliver babies. Now that we had arrived, she would be leaving. All of us talked about how night call would work now that I was there. Martha and Pauline would continue as they had been doing, but I would always be on second call. If they encountered a problem that required help or a question they couldn't answer, they would call me. I told them to call me even if they were getting too tired or just overworked.

Elsie Van Pelt, from Columbus, Ohio, taught at the intermediate school and had been in Somalia since 1964. The mission workers all said, "If you have any questions about the culture or the language, she is the one to go to for help." With her sense of humor and strong communication skills, she knew how to deftly defuse problems among the Somali teachers and students.

I learned at that first meeting that Elsie, like many people, did not feel kindly toward snakes and scorpions. She told us about a time when a large snake lay across the doorway to her classroom and would not budge to let her out for quite some time. Elsie was tall and liked to wear a scarf-like shawl called a *garbasar*. We were told she was an excellent cook who could make any dish she wanted even when she didn't have the ingredients. Elsie did not need potatoes to have mashed potatoes and did not require apples to have applesauce as she could take what was available and make it taste like something else. She taught English and literature courses and whatever else needed teaching, and usually in the afternoon, one could hear her sewing class working the treadle machines.

As I listened to how much work everyone did, I thought there couldn't be time for any tennis, card-playing, reading, beach combing, or just plain socializing. Then I remembered there would be no television, no Jamama morning newspaper, no movies, no sporting events, Lions Club meetings, or even church committee meetings. Maybe there would be some extra time.

By now it was four p.m., and the afternoon was starting to cool off. I had learned that the country pretty well closes down from one to four. It was starting to get busy around the hospital, and I was excited about seeing the facility, meeting the employees, and learning what illnesses and injuries I would be treating. Martha guided me on a tour of the facilities. A front entrance faced the road, but we entered from the back open courtyard. To the right of the courtyard and facing it stood a pharmacy, a supply area, a laboratory, and a patient registration desk. To the left were four examination rooms. On Fridays and Sundays the hospital's clinic closed down as much as possible, but in one room a patient was being examined by a Somali nurse.

Martha introduced him by saying, "Hussein graduated a year ago from our nursing school and has been doing a great job as a nurse practitioner and screener for the doctor. Those patients that he sees and doesn't feel capable of treating he'll send to you with a note on the chart or talk to you about in person."

I asked Hussein, "What disease do you think this patient has?"

"I think he may have leprosy because of these lighter patches on his back and upper arms," he responded. "I plan on his seeing you tomorrow in the clinic."

I then asked if he had told the patient what he thought was wrong.

"No, I haven't," Hussein replied, "because if he has leprosy, he will have to go and live in the Leprosy Colony at Gelib about thirty miles north of here. He will get treatment there, but he will not be happy leaving his home and family. Sometimes the whole family will move into the colony but usually not."

I made a mental note to read about leprosy in my medical books before seeing this patient the next day.

All of the clinic's back area formed a U shape. I asked Martha what a smaller building to the right was used for. "It has two separate rooms that are for the most contagious patients," she explained. "They often accommodate the new TB patients, but now they are both empty." She then showed me an open area behind that building used by families to prepare meals for their relatives who were in the hospital. Water from the mission's well was available as was a place to cook over a fire.

Martha took me into the hospital, where we walked through the male and female wards, each with twelve beds. I observed that the youngest children were in the women's ward. At the west end of the corridor was a rather large surgery room, and at the opposite end, an obstetrical delivery room. Besides the larger wards, there were three double rooms and two private. Although bed sheets were stained and worn, they looked freshly laundered. The faded green halls also appeared clean and the cement floors recently mopped.

The doors of the outside entrance could be closed, but the interior of the hospital, facing the courtyard, was framed by open archways. Large windows allowed breezes to waft through the hospital, but today there was no wind. The air, hot and thick, with an odor of sweat and decaying flesh, took me by surprise, so unlike the antiseptic smell of the Wells Community Hospital that I was used to. Patients' charts hung on a rolling rack that Chester had built, a system that would work well for keeping records.

I was told that we could bypass the hospital restrooms, but I could smell their location. I learned later that each restroom sported a water spigot on the wall, a hole in the cement floor, and a tin can beside that hole. Patients would squat over the hole and use the can of water instead of toilet paper. Except for restrooms at Mogadishu's airport and at the better hotels and restaurants in that city, this was the arrangement Somalis were used to. Some patients from the outlying areas, though, had to be instructed in their usage, since they had never seen a restroom. Martha told me that when patients were too sick to get out of bed, they would use a metal bedpan and family members would be taught how to take care of the waste. Family members would also be taught how to give a bed bath if the patient was going to be hospitalized for any length of time.

Inside the front entrance to the hospital was the office of Hassen Nur, the hospital administrator, a man in his early thirties, neatly dressed and of medium height. Educated in the mission schools, Hassen spoke excellent English. When I asked him to explain his responsibilities, he said, "I manage the hospital personnel and work with you and Martha to agree on the salary guidelines. I take care of the finances to see that all money is collected and that the bills are paid. If you have a problem with any employee, come to me and I will help resolve it. I have worked with the doctors who were here before, and I have been looking forward to your arrival."

I sensed even then that Hassen Nur was going to be a valuable colleague. During the year, he accompanied me to police and government offices, to court, and sometimes to Mogadishu. I asked him to sit in on any complicated discussions with patients or their families. Hassen understood our mission goals and our American attitudes, but he also understood Somali ways of reasoning and thinking. Throughout the year, I was repeatedly grateful for his guidance and friendship.

The other employees and nursing students spoke fairly fluent English and told me how they had been awaiting our arrival. The maintenance personnel spoke only Somali but offered greetings and smiles.

At the end of the tour, I made hospital rounds on all the patients in our thirty-bed hospital. About half of the beds were occupied; that included children who were on fluids for dehydration and several new tuberculosis patients.

My rounds first introduced me to the accident victims who were injured four nights earlier on the road between Kismayu and Jamama. The two women, Fatuma Abdulle Mohamed and Lul Abdurahman Hussein, both in their late thirties, complained of considerable pain when they moved but certainly were not in any critical danger. I reviewed their x-rays and explained their injuries to them Once they realized they would be back to normal after some casting and bed rest, they were relaxed and experiencing less pain.

Then I went to check on Hussein Sadad Hassan, the passenger injured in the front seat of the car. His condition was much more serious. He was alert but weak, with a very rapid pulse and low blood pressure. He looked pale, and his skin was clammy. The nurses had repaired the lacerations, and they looked clean. The fractures were adequately splinted, and he had only mild pain. He told me that he had no appetite but was not nauseated. He had fractured some lower ribs, and I could hear rales in his lung bases that made me feel he could be going into early heart failure.

Hussein was forty-six years old but, like many Somalis, looked much older. He was about five feet eight inches tall, mildly obese, and his hair was already thinning. Neither he nor his family could tell me any medical history except to say he had been healthy. I started him on medicine that evening to slow his heart and make it beat more strongly. He was in atrial fibrillation with a rapid ventricular response. Instead of Hussein's heart having a good, steady beat, the top (atrial) part was beating irregularly and the lower ventricles also beat irregularly and rapidly.

I knew we could not treat him as we would in the States since we could not place him on continuous cardiac monitoring in an intensive care unit. In 1971 the intensive care monitoring and the new cardiac drugs were just starting to reach the rural hospitals in the States and were far from being available in developing nations. I explained the severity of his condition to him and his family, and they seemed to understand. I told them that the next several days would be critical to his survival.

CHAPTER THREE

To know something for sure, one would even part with a she-camel.
—Somali Proverb

Most Mennonite mission workers spend many months or even up to a year in preparation for an assignment. They study the culture in depth, take language studies, and talk with workers who have lived in the area. We had none of this preparation as we embarked on our year in Somalia because, in fact, we had only six weeks from the time we were asked to go to Somalia in June until we arrived in Nairobi in early August.

This is not the way the Eastern Mennonite Mission Board normally functioned. Mission workers were usually well prepared and would often stay in the foreign country's mission headquarters for several months just to experience the culture and learn the language before going to their assignments. In our case, we were going to Somalia because the hospital needed a physician immediately. I would be the emergency fill-in while the board looked for a long-term doctor who could spend one or more four-year terms.

Since we resided in Indiana and the mission headquarters was in Salunga, Pennsylvania, Mary and I never did meet any of the directors except through phone conversations and letters. Making all the preparations to leave our Markle Medical Center practice, getting timely immunizations, arranging for someone to house-sit, applying for passports and visas for a family of five, and packing for a year left no time for any study of Somali culture or language.

We left the States from Kennedy Airport and made our first stop in Casablanca, where we disembarked to stretch while the plane refueled. That was our first look at the desert, and the palms and white adobe buildings reminded me of the famous Bogart film, only this wasn't a movie set. Walking on the northwest edge of Africa, I could only wish for Rick Blaine's easy self-assurance.

Then we continued to Nairobi, our temporary destination. With its roundabouts and a Woolworth Department Store, Nairobi still showed evidence of British colonialism yet looked to us like an undeveloped city. Though the Hilton Hotel rose to the sky, we noticed that it leaned a little. Streets were lined with bougainvillea bushes, flowering poinsettia, and flamboyant trees, but we were startled by the poverty and all the vendors in the market areas who wanted our shillings. Some roasted ears of corn over charcoal fires while others sold brightly beaded necklaces and carvings of elephants sporting small ivory tusks. Beggars abounded and so did people who might snatch a wallet or a purse. However, later, after being in Somalia for seven months and then returning to visit our daughters, we felt Nairobi was a luxurious haven, a Garden of Eden.

Despite some cultural adjustments, we were actually quite euphoric upon our first arrival in Nairobi. Though experts say this reaction is the initial stage of culture shock, our daughters were still with us and so were my parents who had previously been in Kenya for one year, teaching in Kijabe, at a teacher training school. Many of the Kenyans could speak English as well as Swahili, especially when they wanted to sell us some one-of-a-kind wood carving at a special price only for us.

Distinctions in culture and climate were more obvious to us as we landed in Mogadishu. It was hot, stifling hot, as we stepped off the plane and felt heat rising from the cement. Sand hovered in drifts at the edge of the runway, and we felt it swirl around our faces until our lips were dry. We soon discovered that it was often so hot, dry, and dusty that it was hard to get enough saliva to spit out the dirt. The land yielded a few acacia trees and many silver-gray thorn bushes. Along the streets of the city, some oleander shrubs bloomed and an occasional flamboyant tree blazed with orange-red flowers.

We learned that the language we thought the whole world understood got us nowhere. In the entire country, no English was being taught except in the Mennonite mission schools. Mogadishu and the land to the south had all been the previous Italian Somaliland, so some people could speak Italian. Somali, still unwritten at that time, served as the universal, spoken language while Arabic was used for writing and for religious occasions.

Differences between our American culture and the Somali culture spun all around us, and Mary and I realized how intense those differences were during those first days in the country. We did not have that stability gained from knowing how everyone is going to react to your common moves and gestures. Our past experiences seemed like a distant dream.

CHAPTER FOUR

A small path will take you to a big road.
—Somali Proverb

My wife, Mary, grew up on a popcorn farm in northern Indiana, and, before entering the Shipshewana school system, she spent her first five years of education at a rural one-room school where a third of the students were Amish.

Raised in a Mennonite community where signs of worldliness were discouraged, Mary's only jewelry as a girl was a necklace of safety pins she wore behind the spirea bushes where she and her sisters played make-believe. Her first real foray into popular culture came in 1953, when she bought a pair of navy high heels on a home economics field trip to South Bend and then slipped across the street with a girl friend to see her first movie, *From Here to Eternity*.

Until eighteen, I lived at the edge of Shipshewana on a thirty-acre farm. My father was the principal of the high school, but we kept some milking cows which had mostly been my 4-H Guernsey heifer calves, and sometimes we had a few beef cattle along with chickens for butchering. Shipshewana was a small town in which the largest business was the Wolfe Grain Elevator. In grade school a third of my classmates were Amish, too. My first film, like Mary's, was *From Here to Eternity*. While growing up, I never attended a movie with my parents because the Mennonite church in the 1950s taught that movies encouraged the wrong values by showing sinful acts. At sixteen years of age, I felt rather uneasy watching Burt Lancaster and Deborah Kerr "making out" on that tropical beach. It was not a movie I wanted to tell my parents I had seen.

In 1955 Mary and I graduated with the same high school class of twenty-five students, sixty percent of whom were Mennonite. Our Amish classmates had dropped out of school when they turned sixteen, which was usually during the eighth grade. As teenagers in a school with a sizeable Mennonite enrollment, we attended no high school dances and received no class rings. On Wednesday evenings school activities ceased because churches held prayer meetings or midweek services.

At the same time that the pacifist churches we grew up in preached against the worldly pursuits of fashion, wealth, and power, they encouraged us to care about the world outside the borders of Lagrange County. Forks Mennonite Church supported a number of long-term missionaries in Africa and India, many of whom—like Jay Hostetler and Amzie, Orie O., and Ernest E. Miller—were related to me. I looked forward to their return visits when they told stories about people in cultures so different from mine. Missionary families would often share our Sunday noon meal, and while I would be engrossed by their encounters with wild animals and snakes, I also remember feeling so sorry for the poor and hungry children they would describe. I'd ask, "Why do some people have to live in such difficult conditions when we have so much?" I would daydream about traveling to Africa or India to make a difference in people's lives.

Both of my parents encouraged my interest in world history and geography. My father taught U.S. and world history, and every night we listened to world news on the radio with Lowell Thomas. I pored over volumes of *World Book Encyclopedia* and *National Geographic,* studying the pictures of large African game animals and reading about tribal people, their body piercing and elaborate hair-dos. Before my two sisters and I went to sleep each night, my mother read us missionary stories from Africa and India. I admired one missionary, in particular, who worked in Central Africa. I do not remember the title of the book or the missionary's name, but we heard him speak at a conference and bought his book. Afterward, I told my mom, "When I grow up, I want to be a missionary in Africa."

My four years at Goshen College, a school about twenty miles from my hometown, expanded my horizons to some extent. This was a Mennonite college, and I started meeting other students from across the United States and from many foreign countries. The two African-American students who lived on my dorm floor my freshman year came from the inner city of Chicago and became my first friends from a different race. The majority of the full-time students were from Mennonite homes, and I observed that, as a rule, those who came from the Eastern states of Pennsylvania, Virginia, and Maryland were more conservative than those from the Midwest. The differences I noticed in Mennonite culture made me examine my own faith and values and decide what was central and what was peripheral.

In my second year at Goshen, I assisted with the foreign student program and attended its social events. At these festivities the foreign students would dress in their native attire, cook traditional dishes, and talk about their countries. I realized that most of these students were from the upper class and not entirely typical representatives of their countries. Most were supported by wealthy parents, the government, or a mission. Except for a few, they were all Christians who wanted an education so they could return to help the people of their country. But I did not hear much about the physical and social needs of these developing world nations; the students spoke more about the beauty and friendliness of their countries.

When I entered Goshen College, I wanted to become a veterinarian. I figured I would care for animals because I had enjoyed eleven years of 4-H and four years of Future Farmers of America. However, in my freshman year of college, pre-medicine and pre-veterinary students were grouped together and, as I became exposed to the medical field, I realized that my goal had changed. After being away from the farm, I felt less interested in working with animals and more interested in hearing about the health problems of people. The Premed Club asked physicians to speak about the medical field and what it was like to be a doctor, and as I listened, I felt God's tug directing me toward medicine.

Mary and I were married after my freshman year in college. We had been dating since our sophomore year of high school, and, though we occasionally dated others, we always came back together. I loved Mary's beauty—her black hair and bright blue eyes—and her calm, accepting spirit. We had many views in common, and, with similar Mennonite backgrounds, we always had a lot to talk about. Although we knew I had at least eight more years of schooling ahead of me, we had both just turned nineteen; like most individuals that age, we felt we were quite mature.

During the next three years while we lived in Goshen, we traveled almost every Sunday to the town of California, Michigan, to help plant a new church. Our mission team of seven members drove 130 miles round trip to attend worship services and to call on families in this low-income community. During two of the summers, we held a two-week Bible school with an attendance of fifty to sixty children, and after the program on the last Friday evening, parents would comment, "We are so proud of our children. We are going to see that they continue to come to church." For a few Sundays, the children would return, but then, because their parents didn't attend, the children would stop coming, too. While we learned that home missions were not easy to establish, we also learned from our leader, Pastor Melvin Miller, that the fruits of our labors were not ours to judge and that our actions might make a difference for someone whom we would never hear of, a spiritual difference "worth more than any sacrifice of time and money" we could give.

Eighteen months after our marriage, our daughter Shari was born, and now we took on more responsibility. In addition to my college studies, I washed bread delivery trucks on Saturdays, mowed yards and did maintenance work for widows, and worked part-time in Kline's Department Store. I always said that working at Kline's made me study harder because I knew I did not want to spend the rest of my life selling women's shoes.

My attending medical school meant we would be moving to a much larger community. Visiting Northwestern University Medical School in the heart of Chicago gave us a scare. Mass transit, skyscrapers, high-rise apartments, and no family and friends made our interview weekend a nightmare. We didn't think we could make that cultural leap, so we settled on medical school in Indianapolis. Indiana University School of Medicine would be in a much smaller city than Chicago or Cleveland and would be less expensive. However, it was the largest medical school in the U.S., with two hundred students in my freshman class. Compared to Shipshewana, the state capital was an impersonal metropolis. We experienced busy streets with impatient motorists who seemed unforgiving of our indecision and slower pace.

That first Christmas, we drove to the center of the city after our Sunday evening church service to observe the decorations and lights. Indianapolis always trims the downtown Soldiers and Sailors Monument on the Circle like a Christmas tree. The large department stores displayed windows decorated with mechanized reindeer and Santas, carolers, and nativity scenes.

Pausing at a red light a block north of the Circle, we watched an old man with a shopping bag shuffle down the crosswalk. Suddenly, we heard yelling and a man leaped from the car in front of us. He rushed to the elderly man and, with a knife, slashed his neck. The man then retreated back to his car and drove off, as did all of the cars. The old man had fallen to the pavement. Caught in the rush of Christmas traffic, we had to drive away, not able to stop.

By the time we drove around the block, policemen and an ambulance had appeared at the scene. A taxi driver who had seen the assault had called for help. At least we were able to give the police a description of the car and its license number. When we arrived home that evening, we turned on the television and learned that the attacker had already been arrested at his home in a Northside neighborhood. He had stabbed the old man only because he was too slow in crossing the street. Although we felt badly about not being able to stop immediately to help the victim, we felt good about aiding with the arrest. I checked at the City General Hospital a few days later and discovered that the old man had survived and was going to be discharged.

During our acclimation to Indianapolis, it helped that we attended a small Mennonite church with many other young families from rural backgrounds. A caring pastor and his wife, as well as other, older established couples, helped us understand the community and to find our way around the city. For several years I assisted with a ministry to young boys in a deprived section of Indianapolis. I witnessed the boys' unstable family life and their rundown housing, poor schools, and dangerous street life. We picked up the boys on Sunday mornings for church and also took them on camping trips to state parks. That may have been the first time I really saw the effects of poverty on children.

Our parents helped us financially during those four years of medical school. My parents bought a house for us, and Mary's parents kept our freezer full of meat and frozen vegetables from their farm. During the last three and a half years, I was class secretary and treasurer and took notes of all the lectures. After I collected the notes, Mary would type them on mimeograph sheets which I would then run off at the medical school. My classmates bought these notes from us, providing us with enough money so that Mary was able to stay at home with Shari. After taking the notes and then collating, proofreading, and reviewing them, I knew the subjects and diseases well—from anatomy to zooparasitology, from Addison's Disease to Zenker's Diverticulum.

In 1964, after graduating from medical school and spending a year of hospital residency in Fort Wayne, Indiana, Dr. LeRoy Kinzer and I started a medical practice in the town of Markle. Now Mary and I, along with Shari and two-year-old Marlis, were living in a rural community about twenty miles south of Fort Wayne with a culture not too different from the one in which we had been raised. The Amish and Mennonite community in Berne was about thirty miles away, but we attended the local Church of the Brethren.

Five years after moving to Markle and two years after the birth of Stephen, Mary and I, along with Marlis and Shari, took our first overseas trip to visit my sister, Jewel, who lived along the Amazon River in Brazil. Two years older than I, Jewel had graduated from Goshen College with an elementary education degree. After teaching in the U.S. for several years, she flew to Manaus, Brazil, and married Leon Schlatter, a high school teacher with New Tribes Mission, whom she had met in college and with whom she had been corresponding.

From the airplane, Manaus looked like a large, beautiful city, spread out at the confluence where the Negro and Solimoes rivers formed the Amazon. But once we had landed, we discovered many dirt or gravel streets and saw shanty towns where people from rural areas had moved in search of some type of city housing. Unemployment was high and poverty pervasive. We also learned that when you don't understand the language and customs, everything seems dangerous, and people often seem angry when they aren't. In Manaus, even the roosters seemed irate. They would keep us awake with their crowing so we decided that perhaps south of the equator the chickens didn't sleep at night.

After two days in the city, we boarded a wooden launch to take us twenty miles downriver to the mission compound where Jewel's family lived. The barge was soon loaded with Brazilians and the food supplies, cackling chickens, and clothing they had bought in Manaus. We made frequent stops that day to drop off people at their homes, houses built on stilts along the Amazon's edge, and learned that rivers become roads in the rain forest.

During our week at the school compound, we hiked on narrow trails that took us past coiled boa constrictors and alligator pools and into dense vegetation where exuberant species of trees, plants and birds flourished. My brother-in-law took me back in the jungle to visit an elderly gentleman who was sick with multiple problems. I always take some medicine with me when I travel, and I hope that what I gave him helped his illness as I never heard a follow up report.

One day we traveled up a river to a large lake and visited some of the Brazilians living in small wooden houses with tin roofs. Since I spoke no Portuguese and they no English, every conversation had to be interpreted for my benefit. We later docked our boat in the middle of the lake and went diving and swimming. I was concerned that piranhas might attack me and devour a limb or two but was told that they usually confine themselves to tributaries and don't strike unless there is blood.

Visiting Brazil and seeing the work my sister and her family were accomplishing along the Amazon again raised my interest in missions, as did sitting around a kitchen table in the evenings with mission workers from the Indian tribes who asked all kinds of medical questions. Later, when Dr. Victor Binkley, a surgeon, joined the Markle practice in 1970, we discovered that all three of us doctors had an interest in foreign medical work and we spent time talking about how we could respond to this call. We decided that if a request came for one of us to serve a short-term mission stint of up to one year, that doctor could accept it. The two doctors at home would be willing to work harder to carry on the practice, and they would help support the third doctor on the mission field. We also agreed that over the years we would rotate the roles.

Two months after we made this decision, an urgent call came from Eastern Mennonite Board, asking if I could serve as a doctor at Shirati Hospital in Tanzania. We still are not sure how the board obtained my name to make contact, but Mary and I were familiar with physicians who had served or were serving at that long-established Mennonite hospital. Then six weeks after we agreed to go, the mission board informed us we were needed more urgently in Somalia. The board was searching for a long-term physician at the Jamama Hospital, but because none had been found, it needed an interim doctor who could stay for one year—and arrive in six weeks.

CHAPTER FIVE

If people support each other, they do not fall.
—Somali Proverb

The first four weeks for Hussein were touch and go, with one complication after another. He suffered from a malaria-induced fever, intermittent bowel obstruction, and even heart failure. At the end of four weeks, though, his condition was becoming more stable, and he began eating and feeling stronger.

Hussein's large family supplied him with emotional support and brought him meals from the village or prepared them in the cooking area behind the hospital. One of his daughters, who was about fifteen years old, was usually with him. She was quiet, and I could not engage her in much conversation. The oldest son, Omar, also stayed with his father much of the time but would sometimes disappear for several hours or, on occasion, several days, running errands for him. This son, in his early twenties, was always respectful and helpful with his father's care and spoke some broken English. If he had questions, he would ask one of our Somali nurses to translate for him.

Omar told me that his name was a frequent one in his clan. One day as we were discussing Somali names, he explained how the naming system worked. "My father named me Omar after his uncle, and that is the name I always go by," he said. "Then, for the rest of my name, I pick-up the names of all my ancestors, starting with my father and going back as far as I can remember. The first part of my name is Omar Hussein Sadad Hassan Mohammud." Omar was able to go back eight generations, but he said, "Some people can go back fifteen or twenty names."

That day I discovered that Somalis use the first three names only because people from Western cultures usually expect a first, middle, and last name. When Somalis meet someone new and want to establish a relationship, they will start comparing names, and when they arrive at the point where their names become the same, they know how they are related. It seemed to me a good way of establishing a family tree or at least half of a family tree.

Omar explained that girls always followed their lineage through their father. Since Somalia had an oral culture, with the language only becoming a written one on October 21, 1972, the memorization of names from one generation to the next was crucial. This patrilineal kinship system has gone on for centuries and is how Somalis keep such close contact with their clan and how they determine closeness or remoteness in their relations with each other.

Over time, Hussein and I became good friends. I learned that he was employed in the government agricultural program and supervised the southern district. Hussein did not criticize his government but once said, "We have a lot of work to do in our country until we become as developed as Kenya and some of the other African nations. We have started some self-help programs in a few communities, but it is a slow process. My main work now is to establish community water irrigation systems from the Juba River."

"How do you expect to get this accomplished?" I asked.

"We want the villages to build canals off the Juba, and then the small farmers together can construct irrigation ditches," he explained. "We want them to work cooperatively to divert water to their small plots of land during the dry season just like the large Italian banana plantations do."

Hussein did not talk much about his work but enjoyed speaking about past visits to Kenya. When he did this, his eyes lit up, and, though he did not speak in great detail about these trips, I could tell he was impressed with Nairobi and looked forward to returning. I never found out how far Hussein had gone in his schooling, but he mentioned several times how important a good education would be for his children. I also never met his wife, as she now lived in Nairobi.

I had erected a traction device on the third day after I first saw Hussein. We stationed an overhead frame and attached a pulley system with a sling to support his lower leg and put traction on the distal femur. The pulley system extended down to the foot of the bed and ended with some weights. In this way we were able to move him in bed and still keep a constant pull on his femur. The tension helped ease his pain and kept the ends of the broken bones aligned. I also attached a Buck's traction to Hussein's lower leg. This constant pulling stabilized his lower extremity and greatly reduced his pain. Finally, we attached a swinging bar toward the head of the frame so that he could use his arms to pull himself up to help in his bed care. Hussein's health continued to improve, and the bleeding in his bowels stopped.

We really had no way, however, to evaluate the overall status of his heart. Although Somalis rarely had heart disease, probably as a result of their life style and shorter life span, I could tell Hussein had eaten much richer food than the average Somali. The nomads were usually thin and muscular and so were the villagers who farmed small plots of land in the bush. Villagers who had shops or government positions, however, were usually heavier, and, as they aged, they would develop a larger abdomen. Hussein was about twenty-five pounds overweight and had lost much of the muscle mass of his youth. His weight gain was similar to that of the Italians who had lived in

Somalia for many years and who sometimes did have heart disease. Their lives were less arduous than most Somalis and they were, therefore, much less active. They could also afford to buy more meat and pastries.

By the time Hussein had been in the hospital for three months, the x-rays revealed good alignment with the ends of the bones close together. However, there was still no union of the fractured bones, and he was not able to get out of bed and walk. I was surprised by how patient he and his family were at his slow progress. He would say, "It's Allah's will." However, I was frustrated and disappointed in the healing process and had serious doubts as to Hussein's future health.

CHAPTER SIX

What is straight to one man is crooked to another.
—Somali Proverb

As the African-American poet, Amiri Baraka, once put it, "Culture is simply how one lives and is connected to history by habit." The other mission workers in Somalia tried to help us understand Somali culture, but because most of them had served in Somalia for one or two four-year terms, they were so accustomed to the cultural differences that they would forget to tell us how our most common, everyday habits were perceived by the Somalis.

The first thing we learned was that we should never shake hands with the left hand nor give anyone anything with that hand. Touching someone with your left hand is disrespectful; you are sending the message that the person is inferior to you. This was difficult to understand until we learned the history behind that reasoning. In Somalia, the left hand is your dirty hand. For centuries, it has been the hand used to wipe after a bowel movement. Instead of toilet paper, Somalis would use a stone or a stick, but because water is often unavailable for washing, the left hand remains the dirty one. Now the custom made sense. But it was hard not to hand people things with our left hand, and it was particularly a challenge for me since I am left-handed and normally do almost everything with that hand.

During the year we resided in the country, I never once saw a left-handed Somali.

We soon noticed that Somalis never gave a second thought to relieving themselves wherever they happened to be when necessity struck. When riding on a bus, you simply motioned the driver to stop and then ventured outside. Some people would walk to the edge of their village to relieve themselves, but others would go along the streets or on the paths that led to the hospital. We seldom found any public restrooms. Occasionally, at a location like the airport, there would be an enclosure—a small cement pad with a hole in the center to squat over. If we were lucky, there might be a can with some water in it. With her first long-distance bus trip, Mary found that it was inconvenient to travel in culottes because going to the restroom meant she then had to lower her whole outfit, and she might only find a small, dried-up bush to hide behind.

Not knowing the language, we often used motions to help Somalis understand our requests. At first, we pointed with an index finger to what we needed or turned up our index finger and motioned toward ourselves when we wanted someone to accompany us or bring something to us. Again, Somali culture dictates that these actions are very rude because you would only call an animal in that manner. So we learned to turn our hand over with the palm down and move all our fingers inward toward our body, which was acceptable.

It was difficult, though, to change old habits, and I learned to say *kalei jaale* (pronounced *colly jolly*) and to dispense with signals if I wanted someone to come with me but did not know or remember a name. By using the term *jaalle,* which meant "friend" or "comrade," I was actually adopting a word introduced only two years earlier by the Revolution. To weaken clan identification, President Barre's program of scientific socialism encouraged Somalis to use "comrade" instead of words like "cousin," "uncle" and "aunt," terms that applied to those other than brothers and sisters who shared a common descent.

CHAPTER SEVEN

Many words do not fill a pitcher.
—Somali Proverb

Not much news about Somalia ever appeared in the Fort Wayne newspaper or on the television broadcasts we watched. When we stepped off the plane in Mogadishu, we knew very little about Somalia's political situation, though the past decade had been a momentous one for the country. Only eleven years had elapsed since British Somaliland and Italian Somaliland merged to form the Somali Republic, and only two years had passed since President Abdurashid Ali was assassinated by his bodyguards and a military coup brought an end to constitutional government.

Though President Barre would eventually be regarded by many Somalis as a brutal dictator who favored his own clan, in 1971 considerable confidence still existed in the new military regime and in Barre's goal "to restore the pride of our people in themselves and to stimulate a general concern for the greatness of Somalia." In his speech at the second anniversary of the Revolution, Barre answered his critics: "While we have no wish to remain in the saddle of power indefinitely, it would be imprudent to think of a return to civilian rule before our country is ready for it, although that is the ultimate objective."

Barre favored a Soviet-style Marxist government and claimed that the hard work and public service advocated by Socialism was compatible with Islam. At the time we were in Somalia, the government maintained a close relationship with both the Soviet Union and the People's Republic of China, though the former Communist power appeared to wield more influence.

Although we found the majority of Somalis hospitable and felt comfortable in most settings, past events and our status as foreigners and non-Muslims made us feel vulnerable. Therefore, a military government provided us, to some extent, with a sense of security. We did not appreciate, however, all the army personnel with guns at the street corners, airports, and on air flights. Though the government was attempting to foster national pride and support for the regime, frequently the tactics backfired. For example, in September we heard police bullhorns announcing to the villagers that they were required to go the following day to the tarmac road ten miles away and wait for their president to pass in a motorcade. He would be coming through at about ten o'clock in the morning, and they were to wave palm branches and cheer. A representative of the district government came to our hospital and school and told us to give employees a day off and to close the school. The road the next day was lined with expectant people, standing for hours in the sweltering sun without food or water, but, by the end of the day, townspeople came home disappointed and weary. No dignitaries had passed and no explanation was ever given.

The government could be brutal, but more often than not, it just seemed inconsiderate. During our year, we heard of only one time that the military lined up prisoners in front of a firing squad for public execution.

In 1971, the government seemed to be successfully conveying the message that education was an important means for conquering poverty and bigotry. It was building new schools in the larger villages, and our mission schools in Jowhar, Mahaday, and Jamama now had waiting lists for students. These schools invested in the lives of the children, both boys and girls, and I was impressed with the quality of the students I met and by their interest in learning English. Attendance was also high in the adult night school classes taught by mission workers in Mogadishu and Kismayu.

Although Somalia had its National University, the brightest young men from the more prominent families attended schools overseas for their advanced education. Before the Revolution, these men went to universities in Italy, England, or the United States, but in the two years afterward, the only schools these youth were allowed to attend were in Communist countries such as the Soviet Union, China, and North Korea. I asked one man in the government why they made that restriction. He said, "When our young men go to the United States, England, and Italy, they get a much better education, but they never return to Somalia. When they go to a Communist country, they are always watched and sent back."

If the government's early intentions could have been carried out in the economic and political spheres, the last decades might have been much different for Somalia.

CHAPTER EIGHT

What is known is not interesting.
—Somali Proverb

When our destination shifted from Shirati to Jamama, we only knew Somalia's location because our children had a jigsaw puzzle of Africa their grandparents had given them, and the pink Somali piece fit in the upper right-hand corner next to the Indian Ocean and the Bay of Aden.

Before leaving, we did consult our encyclopedia for a general understanding of the country's geography and culture. Of course, we really did not appreciate what we would encounter until we arrived. From the encyclopedia, we found out that Somalia is an African state on the eastern Horn of Africa, with territory that stretches from the tip of the Horn opposite the Gulf of Aden, down like the number seven, in a southerly direction past the equator. It occupies an area of 246,000 square miles, slightly smaller than the state of Texas, and borders Kenya, Ethiopia, and French Somaliland (Djibouti).

Only two rivers in Somalia possess water throughout the year, and both of those are in the southern part of the country where our missions were located. The Shebelle, or Leopard River, flows south toward Mogadishu and courses close to the Mahaday medical clinic and maternity ward. The southernmost river, the Juba, crosses the equator after reaching Jamama.

The Juba and Shebelle usually appear stagnant and muddy, but because they begin in Ethiopia, the speed of the current depends on the rains in that country. Both rivers empty into the Indian Ocean, though for most of the year the Shebelle dries up before traveling that far. The Somalis describe the landscape of the coastal plains, where we lived, as *guban,* meaning "burned," since this area is hot and humid and frequently suffers from droughts.

Seasons in Somalia are classified according to rainy and dry conditions. *Gu* is the first rainy season, generally lasting from March until June. A dry season called *hagaa* follows when winds become stronger and dust clouds develop. The second rainy season, *dayr* begins in September, extending until the dry, harsh season of *jilal* arrives in January.

The history of the Somali people goes back two thousand years to when camel herders migrated from the Ethiopian Highlands and northern Kenya into the Horn of Africa. A thousand years later, these nomadic clans were converted to Sunni Islam by Arabs who had migrated to the coast in the eighth century.

The etymology of *Somali* has not been traced with any certainty. Early explorers claimed the word was a combination of *so* meaning "go" and *mal* meaning "milk it." They noticed that when a visitor arrives at a Somali home, the host will ask a family member to go and milk the animals for the guest. Other writers have argued that the word *Somali* is an ethnic distinction, deriving from a term for a group of Cushitic peoples who live in this area of Africa. I would probably agree with the latter interpretation since no one offered me milk even once during my year in Somalia.

Whenever friends wanted to offer me hospitality, they brought out a spicy, sweet tea called *shai.* Brewed from black tea leaves, sweetened with plenty of sugar, and spiced with cinnamon, cloves, and cardamom, shai was delicious. I particularly liked that it was served very hot, having just been boiled. I felt that, even though the tea looked like water from the Juba, it was safe to drink since so well boiled. Hawa, the cleaning woman in the Jamama hospital, brought me this tea every morning at ten o'clock, and it was the best I tasted the whole year. There may have been something addictive in Somali tea, because I could never get enough.

Somalis are generally tall and slender with soft, curly hair, and skin color varying from charcoal to brownish orange. The nomads present the most typical Somali appearance though today some of that appearance has changed, at least in the cities, as they have married into the Arab populations. The nomads carry with them their convenient huts, consisting of a frame of sticks bent into an arch that can, within minutes, be anchored to the ground and covered with woven mats. These people loved camel's milk. The younger children I saw did well when, after having been breast-fed for a couple of years, they were introduced to that nutritious milk. But one cannot live by milk alone, and the nomads were often short of other foods, especially in the dry season when even camel milk might dry up.

Camels, or *geel,* which can travel for at least fourteen days without water, are clearly the standard of wealth in arid Somalia, and proverbs like "If you have your hand on a she-camel's hump you need not reach higher" express the veneration Somalis have for these animals. Since a camel is considered a man's most prized possession, only a man is allowed to milk it. Important economic transactions such as marriage payments and blood money are calculated by a certain number of camels. In the case of murder, the traditional *mag* or blood compensation paid to the family of a male victim is one hundred camels and, for a woman, fifty.

CHAPTER NINE

The death of a man without camels is no news.
—Somali Proverb

As we traveled the desert roads between Jamama and Jowhar, we enjoyed the sight of camels, often a line of ten to fifteen, moving like pale phantom ships on a sea of sand. We felt part of a timeless world, one that had not changed for three thousand years, since camels were first domesticated. The adult animals would be first in line, bearing the collapsible huts or tents and all the nomads' possessions, while the younger camels followed with their lighter loads. Camel drivers strode alongside the herds, and the rest of the family, also on foot, brought up the rear.

Somalia has the largest population of the world's camels, over five million and all of them dromedaries, the type with one hump. In many countries, camels are no longer so essential to desert life, but in Somalia camels are used not only as beasts of burden but to turn waterwheels and stone wheels that grind sesame seeds into oil. Children are fortunate if they receive camel's milk. It's much more nutritious than cow's milk because it's lower in fat and lactose and higher in potassium, iron, and vitamin C. At the clinic, we encouraged village mothers to give their children camel's milk as soon as they stopped nursing. Migratory families with herds of camels have milk even when they can't reach water, and it is usually safer to drink. Milch camels give two gallons of milk daily, and a large portion of an adult nomad's diet consists of milk.

Camel meat tasted similar to beef, only we found it extremely tough to chew since camels were so prized that they weren't butchered until they were elderly. The normal lifespan of a camel is forty years, and Mary and I figured they must have butchered the camels we ate at thirty nine and a half years. We asked Hawa, our housekeeper, not to bring us any camel meat from the village market, but occasionally she returned with some if there wasn't any other option. Every part of the camel that could be eaten was, and sometimes we didn't know what part we were chewing.

One day a man came into our compound with an elderly camel he herded up the driveway to our house. Mary tried to tell the man that we weren't interested in purchasing his animal, but when he didn't seem to understand, she called me to come from the hospital to explain. This was the oldest, most feeble camel either of us had ever seen, and we felt relief mixed with pity to watch him totter out of sight.

Every part of the camel seems to fulfill a need for the nomad. The hide is fashioned into sandals and blankets, and the hair is woven into clothing. Stomachs provide containers for water, and dung is so dry and hard that it functions as fuel with no drying necessary. No wonder a camel is the Somali nomad's most beloved possession and an essential part of the economic system, with blood money or marriage contracts expressed in terms of the number of camels owed. "A camel is a camel and it is exchanged only for a camel," according to one Somali proverb.

Just the fact that there are forty-six nouns in Somali for camels reveals how revered and important they are. *Awr* or *rati* is a he-camel; *hal* is a she-camel; *rakuub* is a riding camel; *qaalin* is a virgin she-camel . . . and the list goes on. Even urbanites will own or aspire to own camels that kinsmen keep for them in the bush.

I was surprised to discover that, contrary to popular belief, a camel does not store water in its hump. The hump is composed of fatty tissue from which the animal draws sustenance when food is scarce. The mound then becomes flabby and shrinks, and if too much fat is withdrawn, the remaining hump flops from its upright position and hangs at the camel's side. A camel can lose forty percent of its body weight before becoming distressed, a great advantage in a drought.

Camels can also go up to fourteen days without water, and, when it is available, they can safely drink up to twenty-one gallons in ten minutes. They can do this because of a unique metabolism which enables them to store water in their bloodstream. They are also served by a body thermostat that can raise their temperature by as much as six degrees centigrade before they begin perspiring, thereby conserving body fluids.

Though swirling desert sand is a problem for humans, camels come equipped with a thin, nictitating membrane on the eye, like a clear inner eyelid which protects the eye from sandstorms while still allowing enough light to see. A camel's double-row of extra-long eyelashes also aid in keeping sand out. Camels can even close their nostrils to prevent sand from entering their noses, and their large, broad feet do not sink in the sand.

At least several times a month, a caravan with camels camped at the outskirts of Jamama. Within a day or two, a few of the family members would arrive at the clinic. My translator would frequently have trouble understanding their dialect. These patients generally suffered from fewer parasitic diseases than those in the villages and along the river, but tuberculosis was very prevalent as well as injuries and the diseases of aging.

I rarely, though, saw injuries involving camels. People only rode them when they were too ill to walk. Occasionally, a camel would step on a foot by accident, but the usual injuries related to camels were bites. The camel has a large mouth with thirty-four sharp teeth which enable it to tear off tough, thorny bushes without damaging the lining of its mouth. Camels will not usually bite their herdsman, with whom they develop a co-operative, understanding relationship. But when someone else tries to load the camel, perhaps with too large a load, or tries to pull it to its feet too harshly, the camel may show its displeasure by biting or spitting. A camel gulps down food without chewing and then later regurgitates the undigested meal and chews it into cud form. So when a camel spits at you, he is really displaying his displeasure by vomiting.

I found a camel's movements fascinating to watch. Like giraffes, they amble by moving both legs from the same side of the body at the same time. We seldom saw camels run, but I've read that they can reach forty miles per hour in short bursts and sustain speeds of up to twenty-five miles per hour.

When driving, I always gave camels the right of way. There would invariably be more than one, and I would let them all pass before proceeding. They gave no indication they would even consider waiting on me. Besides, a full grown adult camel can stand six to seven and a half feet tall at the shoulders, seven to eight and a half feet at the hump and can weigh nine hundred to fifteen hundred pounds. In 1964, a Mennonite missionary at Jowhar, David Miller, was killed when his motor bike apparently collided with a camel. No witnesses were present, so no one knew exactly how the accident happened.

Unlike the irritating donkeys that brayed outside our bedroom window in the morning, camels made few sounds, and, when they passed by the compound, I enjoyed the song of their wooden bells. Other than some infrequent, high-pitched bleats or bellows, the only sounds I heard camels produce were the grunts and groans they emitted when their drivers attempted to get them on their feet and ready to travel. Now that I've turned seventy, I understand those moans and groans better than I did at thirty-four.

CHAPTER TEN

A broken tradition angers God.
—Somali Proverb

Our greatest cultural adjustment came with understanding that Somalia was a Muslim nation. In fact, it was 99.9 percent Muslim. Most adherents were Sunni and influenced by Sufism, a mystical branch of Islam which entered Somalia in the fifteenth century. We found it pleasant to hear the muezzin, five times each day, calling for the faithful to face northward toward Mecca to pray. Criers called at the first light of dawn, at sunrise, noon, mid-afternoon and sunset. We learned that wherever we were and whatever we were doing when the muezzin called, we could also say a prayer and that the reminder was helpful.

As I appreciated the call to prayer, I enjoyed hearing the children reciting passages of the *Qur'an* (Koran) in the *Duqsi* (Quranic school) next to our compound. The recitation, performed in the school yard, created a rhythmic chant, rising and falling, like the voice of the surf.

Like Muslims elsewhere in the world, the Somalis had prayer necklaces with thirty-three beads that they fingered three times each as they recited Allah's ninety-nine names. These names describe the characteristics of Allah, such as "The All Beneficient," "The Most Merciful," "The All Forgiving," and "The Wise." Muslims hope that, by contemplating these ninety-nine names, they will draw nearer to Allah and develop these attributes in their own souls. But Somalis, like Arab Muslims, believe that there is one name for God that no human knows. Only the camel knows the hundredth, unmentionable name of Allah.

Despite our difference in religion, adult Somali Muslims treated us cordially and never called us infidels, at least to our face. Sometimes, however, groups of children would throw small pebbles and shout "*Gaal*" (infidels) when Mary and Steve went to the market or into the village to visit someone. Though their words could be hurtful, these children never caused physical harm, and perhaps what they wanted most of all was our attention.

On these walks in the town, Mary would see Arab women arrayed in black *shukas* with all but their eyes covered. The Somali women, however, wrapped more colorful cloth around their bodies and left their whole face exposed. Many times these women wore a long, brightly colored scarf draped upon their shoulders or head called a *garbasar*. Somali women never wore pants, though, and, before we left home, the mission board told Mary to pack only dresses and culottes for herself and our daughters.

In 1953 the Somalia Mennonite Mission opened in Mogadishu, and, at that time, Mennonite mission personnel were able to discuss their faith and hold worship services. In the early years a number of young Somalis, most of whom were studying in the mission schools, became Christians and helped form fellowships in Mahaday, Jowhar, Kismayu, Mogadishu, and Jamama. Over the years, however, restrictions concerning religious activities were instituted. In 1963 an amendment to the constitution of the National Assembly of the Somali Republic stated: "It shall not be permissible to spread or propagandize any religions other than the True Religion of Islam." Three months later, all private schools in the country were required to provide instruction in Islam and Arabic, taught by a Somali. At that point, the Sudan Interior Mission closed its elementary schools in Belet Weyn and Bullio Burti, but Mennonites chose to cooperate.

In the 1960s, as Sudan Interior Mission began limiting its activities in the country, Somali believers with ties to that mission or former Protestant missions more or less united under the banner of the Mennonites. But because public worship services were outlawed, it was difficult for these Somali Mennonites to come together and support one another.

By the time of the 1969 Revolution, when the United States consulate was asked to leave Somalia and American business personnel departed as well, the Mennonite Mission was the only Protestant influence in the country other than the Sudan Interior Mission which left the country in 1974. A small Catholic presence remained in Mogadishu due to the Italians who still resided in the country, the first ones having come in the 1880s as part of European imperialism. Mennonites were allowed to stay because of their agreement to provide humanitarian aid in the form of medical and educational services, without active evangelism. The line from a song, "They will know we are Christians by our love," meant a lot to me during my year in Somalia, reminding me that the essence of Christianity is best embodied by acts of compassion and not words.

In 1896, the oldest mission in the country was established by the Swedish Lutherans along the western bank of the Juba River, not far from Jamama (called "Margherita" during the Italian colonial period). Actually, at that time, the territory on the western side of the river was part of Kenya and under British rule. Later this territory was ceded to Italian Somaliland, and, in 1935, the Italian government of Somalia forced the mission to close and deported all missionaries. In 1971 remnants of Swahili-speaking Bantu Christians still resided in that area, and even though we were not allowed to hold public worship services, about six to eight of them would come to our compound to worship in our houses on Sunday mornings.

Elisha was one of the oldest of the group, a man probably in his sixties who was very familiar with the Scriptures. His community would sometimes mistreat him and his family as a result of their religious beliefs, but because they were also of Bantu heritage and not Somali, their religious differences were, for the most part, tolerated. Elisha lived an honest and charitable life in his neighborhood. When a fire caused considerable damage and money was collected to aid those who needed assistance with rebuilding, the community leaders selected Elisha to safeguard the funds because he was considered the most trustworthy person in the village.

During my year in Somalia, several Somali men in their late teens and early twenties asked me to help them in Bible study. They would come to my house after dark, and we would begin our study with the Old Testament stories with which they were already familiar from knowing the Qur'an. In the Islamic tradition, Muslims believe they are descended from Ishmael, Abraham and Hagar's son. They know of Abraham's other son, Isaac, and his descendents; they even know of Jesus, but only in terms of him being a respected prophet. After reading the messianic passages in Isaiah, we would go to the New Testament, where the fulfillment of these Scriptures is announced in the life and teachings of Jesus. In an effort to throw off any government spies, these young men would never come the same night of the week.

Although we didn't share the same religion as most Somalis, we found overwhelming support for our presence and made many friends. The government seemed to take pride in our accomplishments, and there were always many more applicants for enrollment in the schools than we were able to accommodate. Somalis were always observing us and were quick to give assistance when needed. In the hospital, patients and their families were extremely appreciative of our care and treated us with respect. I learned that if I smiled, most of the time they would return a smile. The greeting *nabad miya*, meaning "Is it peace?" was always returned with *nabad waya*, "Yes, it is peace." This greeting dated back centuries and developed as one nomad with his caravan would greet another at a distance, wanting to know if there was amity between them.

We were accorded places of honor whenever we attended weddings, and one example of our acceptance occurred soon after we arrived, when our district, of which Jamama was the capital, celebrated the second anniversary of the military take-over engineered by President Barre. For this celebration in the town square, we canceled clinic hours and school classes so everyone could attend. When we arrived, Mary and I, along with several teachers from the school, were invited to sit on the stage with all the dignitaries. After the program, we were seated for refreshments at the District Commissioner's table.

The Somali workers at the hospital frequently told me what the *wadaad*, or sheikhs, in the mosque had just announced to the people. I can't verify every account. One story I heard at the end of November was that a wadaad in Jamama had announced that a great tragedy would occur in the area unless the people prayed and were blessed. During the next week, ten people would be turned into pigs at night, and five would be from Jamama. That catastrophe could be avoided, the sheikh said, "If Muslims would pray and receive a blessing from me." This blessing, though, like offers of blessed merchandise from some television evangelists, came with a fee. I remember the fear of some Muslim workers during the week after this revelation because nothing in their culture was worse than being transformed into an unclean pig. Others, however, refused to take the warning seriously and laughed.

A Muslim woman in Somalia might be the only wife of a husband, or she might be one of up to four wives. It struck me how difficult the lives of these women sometimes were. I saw injuries caused by wives fighting among themselves or by beatings from their husbands. I never heard any of these women complain, but I know they felt that life had dealt them a hard lot. Although ancient Somali folklore is rich with fascinating stories about powerful Queen Arawello, the Muslim faith and political system gave all the rights to the husbands. As was the case in my own country, until the early twentieth century when women received the right to vote and attitudes toward women slowly began to change, Somali men were the leaders, made the decisions, and had the last word. An old Somali proverb says: "God created woman from a crooked rib, and anyone who tries to straighten it, breaketh it."

Many men, of course, were good to their wives, and some owned homes in several different villages and cities where they would live with a different wife while in that location on business. One day a husband brought all three of his wives and their fifteen children to the clinic for check-ups and immunizations. The nurse told me it was interesting to hear the children, who had never met before and were getting acquainted, talking to each other.

Because Somali mothers do have considerable control over their children—they are the ones who watch them all of the time and are responsible for their development—education for girls will be one of the best methods of improving the future of Somalia.

CHAPTER ELEVEN

Wisdom does not come overnight.
—Somali Proverb

If we had difficulty adjusting to Somali customs, we also observed that the Somalis had difficulty adapting to the introduction of Western technology and culture. For example, most of the Somali people did not understand the power of electricity because it was new to them. There was limited electricity in the large cities part of the time, but most of the country was without power. Our village of Jamama did have a generator that allowed a few businesses to use electricity in the evening.

A year before we arrived, a serious electrical accident in which a number of people died occurred in Jamama. A storm one evening blew down a power line that crossed a street. First, one man who grabbed the wire died. Then someone else coming to pull him away took hold and died. Before the source of the electricity could be shut off, eight to ten people perished, each trying to pull the others from the line.

It was an eerie feeling to drive for miles along the tarmac on the only blacktopped road in our part of the country and not see any lights except for the occasional headlights of another vehicle. Of course, we saw light from the stars. Nights for most of the year were cloudless, and constellations, such as the Southern Cross, seemed especially close. I understood the awe of the stars the Old Testament psalmists felt and why they would see God's handiwork in their movements.

Still, we looked forward to traveling between Kismayu and Jamama when there was a full moon, since we could see some of the landscape and villages. Even then, we always had to be careful to avoid hitting people seated on the side of the road who warmed themselves on cool evenings with heat the tarmac retained. They planned to get off the road before a car reached them but had trouble estimating speed and distance. It did not always help to blow my horn because many Somalis suffered from poor hearing due to untreated ear infections. I drove slower than most drivers, trying not to hit anyone.

The typical auto accident victims I saw at the hospital were pedestrians with both legs broken just below the knees where the bumper crashed into them and with a fractured pelvis where they would strike the hood top. Depending on the speed of the car or truck, they would also receive either shoulder or head injuries from hitting the front windows. You need to realize that Somalis in our part of the country were not accustomed to cars and trucks traveling fast since the road had been paved only eighteen months before we arrived.

People weren't the only ones who had trouble adjusting to the speed of cars on pavement. Animals not used to speeding traffic often failed to get off of the road soon enough; as a result, we treated many human injuries from that type of accident. One night a lorry struck an elephant crossing the tarmac. Many passengers were injured, but no one died.

We knew when we were passing a village at night because we would see a couple of small, flickering lights outside of huts where families might be cooking some broth with vegetables. Most of these villages were not permanent and consisted of five to fifteen houses comprised of palm branches or banana leaves. After a thirty mile trip in the darkness, we were always glad to pull into the compound, where we could see lights from the hospital and homes.

CHAPTER TWELVE

He who is one year older than you has lived in need one year longer.
—Somali Proverb

When I arrived in Caracas, Venezuela, in the 1960s on my way back from visiting my sister's family in Brazil, I noticed the large, attractive buildings in the center of town and the expensive homes around the city's edge. On the hills surrounding the city, the houses grew smaller, less permanent, and less appealing. Our tourist guide explained that the higher you lived, the poorer you were. There was no running water in the hills, and all water and other supplies had to be carted from the bottom. About halfway up, electrical lines disappeared.

Similarly, in Somalia housing arrangements also indicated people's financial situation in the community. Near the center of town, walled compounds surrounded flat-roofed, whitewashed houses that frequently sheltered three or four generations of a family. The most expensive of these homes were built from cement blocks or poured cement with, perhaps, a tree or two to shade them. In Mogadishu many such permanent, cement houses, called *gurgi*, were evident, but their numbers dwindled in Kismayu, and in smaller villages like ours they were rare. In Jamama every house was a single-floor dwelling, but in the larger cities two and three-story homes or apartment buildings were common.

Most of Jamama's better homes had two or three rooms and were comprised of a stick frame plastered with a mixture of sand, mortar and cow dung. Such a house, called a *mundul,* was usually white, but some were the shade of red earth. Though many roofs were thatched with banana or palm leaves, the better houses had tin roofs. The government advocated for everyone to have these because of the great fire hazard of thatch. Whole villages would burn if a fire started when the wind blew.

Furnishings in a mundul were sparse. Wealthy families in Jamama might have bought or inherited some wooden furniture, perhaps a table or an ornately decorated hutch that displayed a few pieces of pottery or china. I never stepped inside the wealthy homes in Mogadishu or Kismayu, but I imagine they were much more lavish. Only a few families in Jamama owned silverware. Large ladles or wooden spoons were used for dipping food onto metal or china plates. The very poor had bowls fashioned from gourds.

Mohamed Aden, a nurse at our hospital, lived along with his wife and two children in a two-room rectangular mundul with no electricity, no running water, and no sewage system. In the bedroom, where clothes hung in a corner, there were two cots, one for him and one for his wife, and several floor mats, woven from banana leaves, for the children. In addition to a wooden cabinet, the other room held a small table with a chair, but I could tell that the family sat on the well-swept floor to eat. Mohamed's wife cooked their food over an open fire in the courtyard, and she washed the family's clothes in the Juba River. Given the difficult living conditions, I marveled at how clean and neatly dressed Mohamed and the other nurses and students were when they arrived in the morning for school or work.

At the edge of a village like Jamama, homes grew smaller; many were just stick houses with thatched roofs. The poorest dwellings were round huts woven from sticks, banana leaves, old cloth, and whatever else was handy. The earthen floor provided only a small space for belongings and for the mats where family members slept. But when you don't know where your next meal is coming from, it's not terribly important to have an investment in real estate.

Somalis, as a rule, appeared happy, and I soon realized that they didn't need things in order to enjoy life. They found joy in their relationships with family and friends. The adults were skilled storytellers, and the children could entertain themselves for hours with something as simple as an old soccer ball. Once, I watched several children rolling an old metal wheel rim with a stick in a game reminiscent of one pioneer children in the U.S. played with a wooden hoop and a stick. I noticed a few old bicycles in Jamama, but otherwise, instead of purchased playthings, children used their imagination to transform common objects, such as sticks and cloth, into toys.

Jamama had no garbage dumps or landfills, and it quickly became apparent to me how little of the earth's resources the Somalis used. In our area, there were few trucks and cars, and the only lawnmowers were goats. Tractors were sometimes required on the larger banana plantations, but even then, the majority of work was done by hand. No factories billowed smoke; most of the waste was biodegradable; and the occasional glass jars or tin cans we saw in the village were recycled for some other purpose. In fact, if we left a tin can or a sack outside, it would soon disappear. We became increasingly aware of how wasteful we had been in the States and how much better stewards we could be of the land and its resources.

After our first few weeks, when we learned that someone else could almost always use what we considered trash, we seldom threw anything away except for the table scraps we took to a backyard pit, where marabou storks rushed forward to snatch them.

CHAPTER THIRTEEN

*A brave man is scared of a lion three times: first when he sees the
tracks; second, when he hears the first roar;
and third, when they are face to face.*
—Somali Proverb

The term *East Africa* brings to mind herds of elephants, giraffes, and wildebeest. It conjures the image of a lion stalking its
prey or a rhino lowering its head. Even if you are going as a missionary, you have your sights set on seeing some African
wildlife.

When we first arrived in Nairobi, our visas for admission to
Somalia had not yet arrived. The mission director, Don Jacobs,
advised us, "Go and see the sights of East Africa, and we will get
a hold of you when the visas get here." So our family took off
toward Mt. Kilimanjaro and the Arusha National Park.

The roads were as dusty as the land was dry and flat as we
drove through Kenya and into Tanzania. Mt. Kilimanjaro,
however, provided a majestic background for herds of kudus,
Grant's gazelles, impalas, and zebras. These animals would be
grazing contently, but you knew they were always alert for
stalking predators. We drove within five feet of a pride of lions,
the young only several months old. Later, we stopped our car to
wait for a cape buffalo to cross the road in front of us. Wild buf-

falo are probably the most dangerous of all the animals we encountered, but, fortunately, they are plagued by poor eyesight. We were not about to challenge this one with our small car; we would have needed an army tank to do that. Most of the land was savanna with tall grasses and thorn bushes, with a wide horizon interrupted by only a grove of flat-canopied acacia trees or a huge baobab, its root-like branches reaching to clutch an incredibly blue sky.

Once, on a small hill near the base of Kilimanjaro, we watched a large herd of elephants with many young ones scattered throughout. The sun was just setting, providing the perfect photo moment. The ranger from the park service who was driving our car through the park suggested we get out for a better picture. Though we knew that, according to the rules, no one was allowed out of their vehicle, with the ranger's permission we walked about one hundred feet to snap some great pictures. As we were gazing into our lenses, the elephants looked up and began walking in our direction. We retreated quickly to the car and waited, as again and again the driver tried to turn the ignition key but to no avail. As the elephants continued to advance, he became increasingly anxious and began repeating, "You had the key—you had the key." Suddenly, he pulled the keys out and threw them at me, shouting, "You drive!" We hurriedly exchanged places, and, with some manipulation to the automatic lock system, I was able to drive away from the advancing herd.

Over the next several days we drove around lakes bordered by pink flamingos and watched as a hyena and a jackal fought over a dead flamingo. We observed small groups of giraffe stretching for the scarce leaves on trees. We shot many rolls of film and could not envision how big game hunters could shoot these animals just for sport or to get the trophy of a horned head for their wall. When we came to the *Ngorongoro* Crater (the Swahili word for "deep hole"), we were amazed to stand on the edge and look down two thousand feet to where herds of wildebeest and zebras grazed on the grass and reeds beside the lake. This crater is the lowest spot in Africa, sometimes referred to as "Noah's Ark" because of all the isolated herds that have lived together for centuries. We saw our first black rhino here and several hippos in a pond coated green with algae. We also spotted our first cheetah and several lions.

Finally, one day when we pulled into the park lodge overlooking the crater, a telegram was waiting: "Visas arrived—return to Nairobi." Our safari was over. It was time to leave Shari and Marlis at their boarding school and for Mary, Stephen, and me to head for our assignment.

In Somalia, we observed many more wild animals over the course of the year but, because of the arid conditions, never in such large herds. We spied warthogs, monkeys, and baboons on most of our road trips to Kismayu, and, when taking the twelve-hour overland trip to Mogadishu, we saw elephants and smaller members of the antelope family, including two kudus that leaped in front of the bus, almost hitting the windshield.

We kept some young wild animals that were brought to our door as pets for Stephen, but he had to be careful to avoid injury as they grew. Most of the time we had two Vervet monkeys, Bonnie and Clyde, tied on long leashes to a wood frame next to our house. When they wanted to be fed, they would chatter loudly or scamper over our tin roof, awakening us in the morning or from a nap.

The word *vervet* means "a cry in the wilderness." These monkeys live in the thorny acacia or fever trees along rivers and streams and forage for insects and tender leaves, thorns and flower pods. Because they raid crops, farmers consider them harmful agricultural nuisances second only to baboons. The Somalis liked to tease us about feeding their pests. Toward the end of our stay, Bonnie and Clyde escaped (or were set loose) and disappeared into the bush. Every few days, though, we would hear them running back and forth on our roof until we'd come out to fill their tin dishes with fruit.

However, we did not do well with ostriches, as the Somalis would give them to us when they were too young. One did survive to be several weeks old, and by then he was able to gain his freedom by outrunning Steve. We also kept one baby baboon for awhile in one of my old shoes. Our dik-dik was only about six inches tall and looked like a miniature deer. We had trouble keeping wild doves but did well with the parrots, Nabad (meaning "Hello") and Nabaday ("Goodbye"), which we kept in a cage on our screened front porch. They were green and a little larger than a crow but not as pretty as those we had seen in the Amazon rainforest.

When wild animals exist in an environment where little food is available, conflicts between humans and animals are inevitable. Animals didn't just eat or destroy Somali crops; they also attacked people. I heard of lions attacking men in the bush, killing or injuring them, but I will describe only those injuries I saw firsthand when victims came to the hospital for treatment.

The worst animal wound I saw was that of a man whose leg had been chewed by a crocodile three days earlier. He had been down at the edge of the Juba River when the crocodile attacked. The leg was laid open and gangrene had already developed. Sadly, he died within four hours of arriving at the hospital.

I cared for two different injuries caused by elephants. The first patient was a forty-year-old man who, while guarding a few acres of maize, was assaulted by a hungry elephant. Farmers had to guard their fields day and night from wild animals; at night, they kept bonfires burning to scare them away. This time, an elephant wanted the grain so badly that it pushed the farmer down and toppled a thorn tree on top of him. He was fortunate to have only two broken bones in his foot, a sprained knee, and multiple deep scratches from the thorn tree.

The other injury was more serious. It involved an eighteen-year-old boy who was guarding his family's vegetable plot. Somalis would try to scare elephants away with sticks and stones, but this usually made them more aggressive. The elephant who attacked this boy used its tusks. One tusk caught the boy's right arm while throwing him in the air, slashing open the forearm and exposing his muscles and some torn tendons. Fortunately, because this boy came to the hospital within thirty minutes of the injury, I was able to surgically repair the forearm and it healed.

It was always helpful for survival and for the treatment of injuries when my Somali patients were able to reach the hospital within six hours of being hurt. Unfortunately, many when injured were days away from the village, in the bush. There were no Good Samaritan helicopters and no ambulances or other rescue units available. Usually, the patient came walking, riding a camel or in the back of a truck. One day a woman arrived, pushed in a wooden wheelbarrow by her husband.

Mary was always more concerned about the danger of crawling animals, such as snakes and scorpions. I saw a few patients who suffered the scorpion's sting and learned that most missionaries, if they stayed long enough in the country, would also experience this excruciating pain. Mary, who was always on the look-out for scorpions and giant cockroaches, swept the house at least once each day and discovered three scorpions in our house during the year. We left the small lizards, a kind of gecko, to cling inside on our screens, basking in the sunshine. They ate mosquitoes, and we were more afraid of those than the lizards. One morning, after Mary arrived at the Kurtz's house to borrow some sugar, she was ready to relax on a sack of flour, when Chester cried out, "Don't sit down!" Nestled on that sack was a good-sized scorpion the brown shade of the burlap.

Our most unusual bug experience came near the end of the dry season: the invasion of the sow bugs. One day Chester commented, "The sow bugs are coming. I saw them down the road by the soccer field, and in three days they'll be at the hospital." These sow bugs were similar to the soft-shelled pill bugs we would find in Indiana when we moved a log or stone in the woods. They liked moist, dark areas away from the light. The sow bugs in Somalia would march at night, covering the ground like a dark, moving carpet. They were supposed to leave if it rained. But we received no rain.

Within three days, the sow bugs engulfed the hospital. They first were seen in the surgery, then down the hall and in the rooms. Finally, they arrived in obstetrics. In the morning, the hospital floor would be littered with dead sow bugs and they'd be swept up, but by evening a new, living mass would creep across the floor once again.

One morning they had disappeared from the hospital, and we knew they were enroute to our houses. Mary put up a strong fight, vowing that the sow bugs would not be entering our home. She packed everything tight and put up as many barriers as possible, including a line of kerosene she poured around the house. We thought all cracks were closed, but within several days, the bugs found a crevice into our house, and we had to sweep them up every morning. In several weeks, they passed through all of our houses and then, with some kind of group intelligence, took the path that crossed the stile into the village. This invasion of sow bugs happened only once during our year in Somalia, but it was an experience as surprising and mysterious as any we had.

CHAPTER FOURTEEN

Do not walk into a snake pit with your eyes open.
—Somali Proverb

Our hospital and clinic in Jamama had a reputation for being a place where patients could receive needed medications, necessary surgeries, and compassionate medical care. No one was denied help. My credentials of general practice and experience with surgery made a good fit for the hospital's needs. However, except for a course on parasitology in medical school, I was unprepared for many of the challenges of tropical medicine in a developing country.

One area of medicine that caught me off guard early in our Somali tenure was the treatment of snake bites. From medical school and medical journals, I knew about poisonous snakes, but the professors and journals had mostly discussed how to recognize the four poisonous snakes in Indiana and where to go for help. In Markle, I never encountered a single patient with a poisonous snakebite, but during the year I spent in Somalia, I treated forty such bites. Patients arrived with snakebites on their legs, feet, arms, or hands.

I would ask, "Was it a poisonous snake that bit you?"

The typical answer was, "A snake bit me, and yesterday two men who were bitten at work both died before they got home."

The men who were bit almost always worked in the banana groves along the Juba River. After the young, transplanted plants were irrigated, the men would wade through the water where snakes might strike their feet or legs. Sometimes, while grafting new plants, they reached their arms down between the banana leaves where a snake would be coiled.

When a patient came to the hospital, the arm or leg would already be swollen and red. I would give a snake antiserum derived from several different species of East African poisonous snakes. We always kept this antiserum on hand for emergencies, with at least one injection reserved for any missionary who might be unfortunate enough to be bitten. Our supplies sometimes dwindled to our last injection, and once we had to use the one saved for missionaries on a hospital patient. There was anxiety in the compound until we secured another shipment, but it did inevitably come in time and no one died for lack of antiserum.

Our supply of antiserum came from Nairobi where, before entering Somalia, my family had toured the serpentarium, observed the many different poisonous snakes, and watched the staff milking them. This experience was just about enough to scare us onto the next plane for the States. The guide tried to reassure us by saying, "There are poisonous snakes all around you every day, but they usually don't bother you, and you don't even notice them. We sent a group of ten of our staff to the Salvo game forest, and they came back with over one hundred poisonous snakes in one day, but many missionaries spend a lifetime in East Africa and never see a live snake."

Most of the snakebites I treated were probably from the green mamba. This slender, emerald snake blends well with the banana leaves and grasses. But the Somalis did not differentiate between snakes. Their word for snake is *cobra*, so when I first arrived, I thought everyone was being bitten by actual cobras.

When snakebite victims came to the hospital, I would mark their arms or legs to indicate where the swelling extended when they first arrived. After we gave them the antiserum and cortisone intravenously, the nurses would add a mark every thirty minutes to show the advancement of the swelling, warmth, and redness. Usually in four to six hours the swelling would stop advancing. At that point, we knew the patient would recover.

The only patient that year who didn't recover from his snakebite was Aden. This twelve-year-old boy was brought in from a small village ten miles from the hospital. It was a hot day, and when his father carried him into the hospital, Aden's right arm and chest were already swollen tight. His face was so puffy it appeared to be blown-up like a balloon.

I asked the father what happened and, through my nurse interpreter, he said, "My son was out in the bush at the edge of the village when he was bitten on his hand by a cobra. The same snake then spit in his eyes, and the other boys with him brought him home."

This was the only snakebite incident we had all year in which a patient encountered a spitting cobra. We immediately gave Aden intravenous cortisone and the East African snake antiserum, but his respiration had become labored. Just as we were preparing to perform a tracheotomy, Aden stopped breathing and his heart stopped.

To see a twelve-year-old boy die so suddenly was hard for all of us to handle. His mother screamed and wept, and, when we tried to console her, she was calm for a few minutes but then screamed and cried again. I offered to drive Aden and his parents to their home if she would try to control her emotions. She sat stoically in the Fiat except for when we passed through several small villages. Then she would thrust her head out of the window, unleashing a high-pitched wavy screech followed by loud sobbing. I felt sorry for her loss, and I understood her need to let everyone know the intensity of her grief.

At home, we always watched our step so as not to be surprised by a snake or scorpion. The nurses at Mahaday told us how they were awakened one night to the clatter of pots and pans, the disturbance caused by a large snake scaling the kitchen wall. In Jamama, a teacher felt trapped in her classroom as a snake lay across the threshold of the door. Our first task, when we arrived at our house in the compound, was to find ways to fill all the cracks in the walls and to repair all the screens. Mary made sure that our final inspection was thorough and complete.

Our best snake story occurred one Sunday afternoon when we were at the post office getting the mail, always one of the highlights of the week. Mail would arrive on Thursdays and Sundays although many weeks it never came at all. That Sunday, a lorry, a truck with an open bed, drove up to the post office, pulling a huge python. I stepped off the dead snake and found it to be sixteen feet long. About one-third of the way down its leathery body was a significant lump. The driver said the python had devoured a small goat before they could kill it. This experience literally added a new dimension to our concept of "snake."

CHAPTER FIFTEEN

He who does not shave you does not cut you.
—Somali Proverb

I have always felt that I should send my patients to where they could get the best possible medical care for their particular illness. When coronary artery bypass surgery first became a treatment for coronary artery disease, I sent my Indiana patients to Cleveland Clinic Hospital 250 miles away because it boasted the best program and results in the Midwest. Within two years, Indianapolis Methodist Hospital was on a par with Cleveland Clinic for coronary surgery, so then our patients had to travel only ninety miles to get comparable care. Now, for the past twenty-five years, our patients have traveled only twenty miles to Fort Wayne for topnotch cardiac care, including heart transplants.

Since I have always been conscientious about where I send patients, it might seem strange that I would perform cataract surgery in Somalia when I had not been trained for it or even observed a cataract surgery.

Soon after I arrived, I was told that Dr. Ivan Leaman, the first doctor at the Jamama Hospital, did many successful cataract surgeries during the second term of his tenure from 1960-69. Patients still traveled to our hospital because they had heard, "You can get your eyes fixed so you can see again at the Mission Hospital." When patients arrived totally blind or nearly blind with cataracts, our Somali nurses asked me to help them because I was a doctor.

In the States it would be considered malpractice for me to perform an operation for which I had not been trained. So initially I said that under no circumstance would I operate on cataracts. I tried to locate a place to send patients for the surgery but discovered that no one in all of Somalia was removing cataracts. Mohamed Aden, one of the Somali nurses, told me, "Two years before you came, an eye surgeon from China performed cataract surgeries in Somalia. He did about fifty operations a week for a month before leaving. However, when he was finished, not one of the patients could see."

I didn't know if this was the absolute truth or if Mohamed was stretching the facts to persuade me to reconsider my refusal, but it was hard to deny help to those who could not see when I knew that, in most parts of the world, removing a cataract is a minor procedure. Blind patients would come to me, saying, "I cannot see now because I am blind. If you operate and I cannot see, then it is God's will. If you operate and I can see, I will be forever grateful to you." I began to pray fervently for those patients and for the direction I should go.

I discovered a book in the hospital describing how to perform cataract removals and a four-page typewritten procedural form in the doctor's file cabinet, both of which I started studying. Mohamed, who later assisted me with the operations, rounded up all of the surgical equipment except magnifying glasses. In the storage depot, we uncovered a box of unused, thick cataract glasses sent from Kenya when Dr. Leaman was performing removals. The box read, "One size fits all." After surgery, patients would need these glasses to take the place of the lens that would be removed from inside their eyes. Without the glasses, they could see, but nothing would be very clear.

In 1971 cataracts were still being removed by creating a corneal flap, taking out a section of iris and then breaking the fibrous attachment and removing the hardened lens (the cataract). The cornea would then be closed with very fine interrupted sutures. Several drops of saline would be placed in the space where the lens was located, and the cornea would be made smooth as possible. Patients would stay in the hospital for two to three days with sand bags beside their heads to limit movement. Several weeks later, they would be fitted with cataract glasses.

Our procedure at Jamama was the same as in the States. I reviewed the surgical steps so often in my mind that I felt I had already performed the procedure.

My first cataract patient was Miriam, a woman who didn't know her exact age but was probably between sixty-five and seventy and had been totally blind for several years. To reach us, she and her family had traveled from the bush area near Baidoa in a small caravan, a trip that covered about 300 kilometers over eight days. This was in late October, about two months after we had arrived. I tried to explain to Miriam and her family what I was going to do, but they, like most of my Somali patients, showed little interest in knowing the details. They were putting their trust in me. The prayer we had with Miriam at the surgical table helped alleviate my anxiety about how the procedure would go.

I injected an anesthetic around her eyelids and used a retrobulbar injection to paralyze the eye. This second procedure was accomplished by inserting a long, thin needle and angling it from the outer lower margin beside the globe of the eye to behind the eye where the large nerves are located. During the surgery, I used a small magnifying glass that Stephen had brought with him from the States, part of a toy chemistry set. After the surgery was finished, an hour and thirty minutes later, we applied an antibiotic ointment and an eye patch with an eye shield and took Miriam to a hospital bed.

Two days later, family members and nurses gathered around Miriam's bed as I removed the eye patch and shield. I cleaned the eyelids and asked her to open her eye and tell me if she could see. Her first words were, "You are white. I can see." A big smile spread across her face. Now she could see her children and grandchildren. She would be able to watch young goats nurse from their mothers and see the wildflowers bloom in the desert during the rainy season. Since the Somali language was an unwritten language, Miriam didn't need vision for reading; she was overjoyed with the results of her surgery—although they would not have been acceptable in the States, where reading is such an integral part of our enjoyment and existence.

Soon we had a long list of patients waiting for cataract surgery. I started doing one or two each week. Even though patients would want their second cataract removed after the first one had been successfully taken out, I insisted that they wait and allow someone else the opportunity to see. My feeling was also that someone better trained would come along in the future and do the surgery more effectively and easily than I could. I also never performed surgery on anyone who was not totally blind. I remembered the Hippocratic Oath and its tenet to do no harm. All twenty-eight of the cataract patients were able to see when we were finished.

That was fortunate, since it is much easier to remove a cataract before it becomes overly mature or ripe. When the cataract is too mature, as most of those I removed were, it is hard to extract the lens intact. The lens grows soft and breaks up easily, leaving particles in the anterior chamber that interfere with vision.

On my tenth patient I did have a complication. If it had happened on my first surgery, there probably wouldn't have been a tenth or even a second. I was injecting the anesthetic with the long needle to the back of the eye when, suddenly, the eye popped forward and out of its socket! Fortunately, I had read about the possibility of this happening in the textbook. I immediately applied pressure on the eye and held it there for fifteen minutes. Then I placed a pressure patch over the eye and sent the patient to a hospital bed. The next day I removed the cataract on the other eye without any problem.

Twenty-eight patients regained their sight, but that's a very small figure when you realize the number of blind people in Somalia. Each patient was overjoyed at being able to see again, and families appreciated the help the hospital provided for their loved ones. I had approached the first operation somewhat blindly myself. Because I did not already have the skills to perform the surgery, I depended on what I could read from others who had successfully removed cataracts. I also depended on a Somali for medical guidance. Mohamed Aden, a nurse with entry level training who had previously helped Dr. Leaman during many cataract surgeries, explained some of those same procedures to me and stood at my side. If I was willing to receive instructions from others, then I could be God's instrument to bring sight to the blind.

CHAPTER SIXTEEN

If you have managed to avoid a premature death, you will not manage to avoid old age.
—Somali Proverb

In the States we see the fragility of life in the untimely death of a teenager who falls asleep at the wheel or of a middle-aged woman who succumbs to breast cancer. But in developing countries, where lives are also very precious, a much narrower band exists between life and death.

When a person's body is already weak from malnourishment and possibly from an underlying, chronic condition such as tuberculosis, an acute contagious virus or parasitic infestation can abruptly end a life. For Somali children, acute diarrhea with dehydration or an acute malarial attack is commonly fatal. A survey in the Jamama district taken two years before we arrived revealed that of the children who reached one year of age, only half reached age fourteen. Because the first year of life was particularly dangerous, some babies were not named until several months old. It was not unusual for a woman to have experienced eight or nine pregnancies with perhaps six live births and yet be left with only one or two living children.

For the healthy adults who made it through those dangerous childhood years, the period between fifteen and fifty years would be the safest—though for women a lack of prenatal care and trained midwives resulted in a high maternal death rate. Older individuals would sometimes suffer from such diseases of aging as arthritis, back pain, hypertension and, in rare instances, diabetes.

It was hard to actually ascertain the age of the elderly. I might ask a man from the bush his age, and he would speak to my nurse interpreter for quite some time until finally the nurse would just shrug her shoulders and remain silent. When I would insist on knowing what was said, she would say something like, "He claims he is one hundred and ten years old, but I know he isn't that old. He counts his years by the number of rainy seasons he has lived through. Most years there are two rainy seasons, but some years there are none or, like this year, only one. He's from the bush, and he really doesn't know how old he is at all." I soon stopped asking the age of the elderly; it took too much time and seemed futile anyway. In general, the older people in a family were well cared for and respected. They would have persevered through hard times, but they seldom complained.

We treated critically ill patients in the hospital, but with only thirty-six beds in a district with thousands of people, our efforts sometimes felt like a drop of water in the desert. In the clinic, we were able to see many more patients and provide them with some health instructions and preventative medical care. However, we were dependent on patients coming to our clinic, and usually when they came, they were concerned about a specific problem. The nurses and community leaders told me that in the ten years the hospital had been in Jamama, they could see a remarkable improvement in overall health. But there were hundreds of smaller villages scattered along the Juba River and in the bush that received no medical care.

In the early 1970s, the United Nations declared Somalia the last country in the world to be free of smallpox, with the last case appearing in the late 1960s. In league with UNICEF, our clinic helped to vaccinate everyone in the Jamama area against the disease. But so many other contagious illnesses needed to be eradicated. How much better it is to prevent an illness than to treat it when it occurs. Usually it is also less expensive to immunize hundreds of people than to treat just one individual who suffers from the disease. We experienced this in the States, when Dr. Jonas Salk developed the immunization for poliomyelitis in the mid twentieth century. I lost several cousins to polio in the 1940s and '50s, and throughout the years I have treated patients with complications from the disease. Fortunately, children and young adults in the States will never experience our fear of polio. But this disease is still a problem in much of the world where people have not been adequately vaccinated.

Those of us who worked in the Jamama clinic and hospital realized in 1971 how important a public health care outreach program with immunizations would be in our district, but we faced many obstacles in carrying out an effective plan. The villages, many without names, lay scattered, and some of the smaller ones continually relocated, as did the nomads. Before we could start any program, we needed to locate the villages and obtain the approval of the elders. Furthermore, not the least of the difficulties was getting the financial support to carry out our goals. As with any public health program, there was never any income, only expenses. Some immunizations we could obtain free from UNICEF, but others we had to purchase. Eventually, we scraped together some funds from the hospital budget and also acquired money from churches and individuals in Indiana. After a day of immunizing villagers, I recall coming back enthusiastic about the good we had accomplished and eager to go full time into public health.

The typical village we would immunize might have fifteen to thirty homes in a clearing in the bush. If villagers were fortunate, they might enjoy the shade of one or two acacia trees. We would park our Fiat near the edge of the village and walk toward the center, looking for someone who might be a chief or an elder. Often a group of elders would be seated in whatever shade there was. We knew we could not be pushy and must take our time. After introducing ourselves, we would tell the elders or chief where we were from and the purpose of our visit.

Occasionally, someone would step up who had been to the hospital or the clinic. This was always beneficial since the person would speak of how he or she, or perhaps a son or daughter, had been made well through our efforts. We explained how the shots would help prevent diseases and emphasized how other villages were getting them because they wanted to prevent illnesses and deaths. Sometimes the elders would invite us for tea, and I could usually feel the tension lessen as we continued our conversation without being too insistent.

When the elders gave the word that they wanted everyone in the village to receive the immunizations, the people would begin lining up, eager to be among the first. As we gave the shots, we glimpsed the older children running to find and catch the three- to six-year-olds who wanted no part of the program and so were often brought to us kicking and screaming. The villagers, who loved one another with a strong clan bond, were careful that not one individual be missed. Tetanus, diphtheria, polio, cholera, hepatitis, and measles were killing so many of their infants and young children, just as earlier these diseases had killed many in American communities. For instance, my own father, while growing up, lost a teenage brother to tetanus and another brother to an infected leg injury.

In October at our hospital, a baby boy was born whose mother died soon after giving birth. This was always a tragic situation, but even more so in Somalia, where a baby who isn't breast-fed rarely survives. The father realized how tenuous the baby's situation was and asked if we could keep his son in the hospital.

Since a hospital is not a good place to raise a healthy child, Mary and I, with the father's permission, brought baby Abdi to our home. For the first ten months of his life, he was a part of our family. He was, in fact, the healthiest infant I saw in Jamama. Mary would explain to Abdi's aunts the care she gave him, and she would take him to the nursing school where the students would observe how she bathed him, pasteurized his milk, and boiled his water. Abdi received his immunizations on schedule and started solids. Stephen bonded well with Abdi, and this was his opportunity to have a younger brother.

CHAPTER SEVENTEEN

People pray to Allah differently, and they speak differently.
—Somali Proverb

While we were in Jamama, Ramadan occurred during the last week of October and the first three weeks of November. This period of fasting, established in 638 A.D. to mark the month in which the Qur'an was revealed to the Prophet Muhammad, begins with the sighting of the new moon in the ninth month of the Islamic calendar. During Ramadan, every able-bodied Muslim is to refrain from food, drink, and sexual relations from sun up until sun down.

Thinking about the ambiguity of twilight, I once asked Hassen Nur, "How do you know exactly when the sun has gone down?"

"We know the sun has gone down when we can no longer see the hairs on our forearm," he told me.

Then everyone would feast and drink. They stayed up late at night and rose early in the morning, before it was light, to eat a large breakfast together as a family.

The fourth pillar of Islam, Ramadan is considered the most venerated, blessed, and spiritually beneficial month of the Islamic year, but at first I found it very intrusive because everything operated on just half a schedule. Our hospital employees and students who were fasting could do little in the afternoons because the hot, dry conditions made them feel faint. In fact, they were often so weak and exhausted they had to return home. I also was disgruntled by the fact that some observing Ramadan took the prohibition against drinking so seriously that they wouldn't swallow their own saliva. Some patients brought cans or cloths to spit their saliva into, but others would simply spit on the hospital floor or walls.

But when I learned the meaning of Ramadan, I started to admire the participants for their persistence in keeping it. In addition to fasting, participants pray, perform acts of charity, and look inward to observe self-accountability. They are encouraged to read the entire Qur'an during the month, and special prayer services, called *Tarawih*, are observed in the mosques every night of the month during which an entire section of the Qur'an is recited. In addition to refraining from food, drink, smoking, and sexual relations during the day, Muslims are expected to exert more effort into following the teachings of Islam, avoiding anger, envy, greed, lust, sarcastic retorts, backstabbing, and gossip. The act of fasting itself serves to redirect the heart away from worldly activities and to cleanse the inner soul. This was all to be lauded, and it reminded me of the Christian period of Lent that starts with Ash Wednesday and extends until Easter Sunday. Like Ramadan, this is supposed to be a period of self-sacrifice and introspection.

October and November should have been the rainy season, *dayr*, but that year we experienced only ten minutes of rain and few cloudy days. It remained hot and dry. The temperature would range from over 100 degrees during the day to the 80s or low 90s at night. Without the rainy season, there were no crops and the cattle and goats appeared bony and haggard. With Ramadan coinciding with all this heat, the clinic and hospital became more chaotic, with an increase in patients and a decrease in people to help. There were fewer routine clinic visits but more new, critically ill patients. People who were healthy and controlled their activities tolerated fasting without difficulties, but those who were already ill became acutely debilitated. We saw many new tuberculosis patients since fasting and dehydration pushed them to seek medical help. Many times these patients were carried to our clinic by family members. A large proportion of the new patients were nomads who had traveled a long way to seek treatment at Jamama.

The most difficult problem was getting patients to take their medicine during Ramadan. Some would take liquid medicines and pills without water, but others refused to take any medicine and would not even allow us to administer an injection. Some medicines could be given all at once or twice daily, but in 1971 we didn't have access to many long-acting medications. We tried to accommodate most of the patients, but those sick with high fevers, perhaps with acute malaria or pneumonia, required intense and immediate treatment. Fortunately, our nurses or the religious leaders in the community could usually convince these patients of the critical nature of their illness and that it was acceptable for them to take treatment because they were not able-bodied. God would not hold it against them.

Most of the time we did not have problems with the children as their parents would allow them to take medicines and drink liquids when we explained their importance. Breast-feeding was always allowed and most children would not fast until six years of age. Some, not until puberty.

CHAPTER EIGHTEEN

A madman does not lack wisdom.
—Somali Proverb

It wasn't until early November that I finally found time to leave Jamama and make my rounds of the other mission compounds. This meant finally getting to Mahaday to visit Velma and Anna, the two nurses with the maternity ward and busy outpatient clinic. They were performing an outstanding medical service, but new problems had arisen, and we needed some time to work them out. For the treatment of some diseases I brought an updated protocol and also medical supplies from the hospital. We spent time that first day in the clinic discussing treatment options for some of the most difficult cases.

In the evening after supper, we continued our medical discussions. At one point, Velma said, "Anna and I have made several visits to see a young woman named Fatama who is chained up in her own house. Her family has asked for our help, but we don't know how to treat her. Her husband told us she was okay until after the birth of her baby, her first child. She has shown no interest in her baby and has started screaming and becoming violent with her husband and family. We have tried to give her something to calm her down, but she just keeps spitting the pills out." Velma asked if I would go with her on a house call the next morning to see Fatama.

The Mahaday compound was located along the Shebelle River. That night it was moonless with unusual cloud-cover, since we had not had any rain for quite some time. About midnight, I awoke to loud yelling in the village. Looking outside, I could not see any problem, but I did notice that Leon Good, the director of the mission and of a community agricultural project, had left his house in the Land Rover. Soon it quieted down, and I went back to sleep.

In the morning, Leon told me that the guard watching all the village gardens had set off the alarm because a hippopotamus had emerged from the river and was foraging the half-grown crops. In past years, the hippo would have been shot, but now it was chased back to the river with loud cries, sticks and stones, and the lights from the Land Rover. Before the Revolution, Somalis carried guns for hunting, as did the missionaries, but since then, only soldiers were allowed to own firearms.

After breakfast, Velma, Anna and I left the mission on foot to see Fatama, the woman whom the Somalis deemed possessed with demons. The village was abuzz with talk about the hippo that had trampled the gardens. We made our way down dirt streets, followed by an increasing number of young children. Finally, we arrived at a small, round house with walls of sticks, mud, and cow dung and a cone-shaped roof thatched with banana and palm leaves. The fence that enclosed this house and a few other houses of the same compound was composed of sticks tied together with old wire.

Fatama's husband came out of a house and greeted me. He said, "I have been praying to Allah for help for my wife. I am so glad you have come." Together we entered the one-room house. Inside, the only furnishings consisted of a wooden chair and a banana leaf mat, but the dirt floor was well swept. A small tin dish rested on the floor but no utensils.

The woman, who appeared to be in her late teens, lay sleeping, without clothes, near the dish. She was thin, coated with dirt, and her hair was matted. "We cannot keep any clothing on her," Fatama's husband said. "She mostly crawls around on all fours and eats by putting her face in the dish." She was chained by her ankle to a stake.

As I walked further into the room, Fatama sat up and stared at me. She tried to reach me, stretching out her arms in a non-threatening manner. At the same time, she seemed to speak to me in Somali as if explaining her problems. I asked the nurses to translate.

Anna replied, "It's just mixed up syllables and means nothing. We can never understand anything she says, and her husband says she has been like this for the past six months." Fatama stared at me, her eyes, piercing. She kept reaching for me as if begging for help.

This woman had obviously lost contact with reality and could be described as having a major psychosis. I had read about patients in Europe and the United States who exhibited this type of behavior before the advent of antipsychotic medications. In fact, I had observed a few such cases in the early '60s when, during my medical training, I toured several Indiana mental hospitals. The nurses and I felt a deep compassion for this young woman and her family. I recommended we obtain a medication called Largactal (thorazine) and have the nurses give her an injection twice each day. If she improved, we might then be able to give it to her orally.

The next day I went shopping in Mogadishu for Largactal. The pharmacies were one-room shops with counters that separated customers from the medicines. No prescriptions were ever required since all you needed to purchase any medication was enough shillings. I went to three pharmacies before I found one with injectable Largactal. Different pharmacies bought medications from different countries, and the medicine I bought was from Italy and had an Italian name. The pharmacist had a three-week supply, so I bought his inventory and told him the nurses would come for more. Because I requested all of his vials, he offered a reduced price, but, because I was an

American, I probably still paid more than others would have. Bartering was not something I enjoyed, and I didn't mind paying a little more than everyone else if the price was reasonable.

Velma and Anna reported to me that Fatama did gradually improve. We kept adjusting her medication, and in three weeks she started taking it orally. A couple months later I saw her in the clinic with her husband. She was well dressed and looked much healthier. She had lost her wild-eyed appearance and could not remember the psychotic life she had lived. But her husband remembered, and he was very thankful that his wife was well again. I wondered how many others in the country lived in chains, without any hope of psychiatric care.

In Jamama, there was a young man in his early thirties named Ibrahim who roamed through the village, preaching. The Somalis told me, "Ibrahim is crazy in the head. He is telling everyone they must not have their boys and girls sleeping in the same room at night. They must have individual bedrooms and must have inside toilets so they won't be seen urinating or defecating. Also, he says that no man should have more than one wife." Ibrahim's injunctions collided with village culture, and even if they wanted to, families could not economically afford the changes he was preaching. Villagers just laughed at Ibrahim and called him crazy.

"Why does Ibrahim talk about these things and when did it start?" I asked Abdi, one of our graduate nurses.

"Ibrahim is the son of the previous ambassador to the United Nations," he said. "He lived in New York City for four years, and when he returned to Jamama all he could talk about was how everyone needed to live like people in New York. Of course his message was not well received and people started laughing at him. Now he has withdrawn from everyone and hasn't worked since returning. The villagers agitate him, trying to get him talking so they can laugh."

Ibrahim would hang around the hospital, but I could not get him to speak to me. In fact, I learned that he could speak very little English for having spent four years in the States. He lived with his mother while his father worked in Mogadishu, and he was always clean and well dressed. His thoughts, though, seemed far away, and he wore a dejected expression. Ibrahim certainly suffered from depression, and I don't know if he really was in contact with reality. I never gave him any medical treatment, but I saw how shifting between cultures had messed up his life.

One day a twenty-one year old man was brought to the hospital by friends after he had taken a swallow of DDT concentrate. Within thirty minutes of his having swallowed the poison, we had pumped his stomach empty and washed it out. The police entered the hospital shortly after the patient had arrived. "We will keep a guard by his bed until you release him," the captain said.

"That won't be necessary," I told him. "Our nurses can keep watch over him."

I then learned something about Somali law when the captain replied, "We are watching him so that he doesn't escape. When you release him, he is going to prison. The penalty for attempted suicide is six years."

I thought it was good the penalty for attempted suicide wasn't being put to death. I came to understand, though, that six years of incarceration was almost comparable to a death sentence. Food supplies were scarce in the prisons, and many illnesses, especially tuberculosis, were rampant.

It was hard treating those with anxiety and depression because I had difficulty with the language and the Somalis had no words for these illnesses. I mostly had to inquire about their symptoms. Anemia from a hookworm infestation or a cough from tuberculosis was much easier to treat than fatigue and low self-esteem. It was easier to give children money for food or milk than to treat a mother's postpartum depression. We had an abundant supply of powdered milk and penicillin, but no medicine for mental illness.

CHAPTER NINETEEN

*Let what is on this side of the bank be washed out by the flood and
what is on that side of the bank be carried away by the wind.*
—Somali Proverb

Since the day Hussein was admitted to the Jamama hospital, I
had tried to talk his family into transferring him to the government hospital in Mogadishu when he stabilized. He was a
highly visible government employee, and I assumed this hospital would have orthopedic surgeons and provide the country's
best health care. But Hussein's family refused, stating, "If he
goes to the government hospital, he will surely die."

Later, I did visit this hospital and was startled by its large,
dirty rooms and patients with open wounds or hooked to
empty IV bottles. In the hall outside one ward, several dead
bodies lay sprawled on the floor. It reminded me of conditions
from the Middle Ages. Hussein and his family would agree to a
transfer to a hospital in Nairobi, but the government refused
permission. Then, in early November, I received a telegram
from the government in Mogadishu, stating that I must operate on Hussein's leg so it would heal. It also stipulated that the
operation was to take place in the next several weeks.

Dr. Urquhart, a Canadian-trained physician in his early
fifties who had been in East Africa for many years, ran a small

clinic in Kismayu and also one in Mombasa, Kenya. Several times I had given anesthesia at his Kismayu clinic when he was performing surgery and had consulted with him about Hussein's condition and care. I again sought his advice about the government's telegram. He said we should perform the surgery. He had a patient from the city of Aden in Yemen with a metal rod in his leg that he wanted removed. We could remove that rod and place it in my patient's leg. First, I went to his clinic and gave a spinal anesthetic to his patient while Dr. Urquhart removed the rod. We then arranged for surgery on December 14 to insert the rod in Hussein's femur.

We began this surgery at about one p.m. at the Jamama Hospital. I administered the anesthetic, and Dr. Urquhart performed the operation. Everything went as planned except for excessive bleeding at the incision site. There was a lot of granulation tissue around the fracture, and his flesh was of poor quality since he had been confined to bed for over three months.

The surgery was completed around three-thirty, but we knew Hussein's condition was poor. He was in shock, with a rapid and weak pulse and cold extremities. His blood pressure and blood count were very low. We gave him medicine to raise his blood pressure, but it refused to rise. We also sought to give him blood. However, Hussein's blood type, B positive, was rare among Somalis, and no match was found among his children, the hospital employees, or the missionaries—except me.

That evening I gave two units of my blood. His blood count improved, but he remained in shock. I kept feeling inadequate to help him and knew that if only we had the medicine, facilities, and specialized care available in much of the developed world, we could have changed the course of events.

Although Hussein could breathe on his own, he never obtained full consciousness. A day and a half later, he died at five in the morning with his children at his side. The nurses carefully wrapped Hussein's body in a sheet, and the children took their beloved father home for anointing and burial.

PART TWO

"Love emerges when hands give something to each other."

—*Somali Proverb*

CHAPTER TWENTY

Every prayer should be offered at its proper time.
—Somali Proverb

Since Hussein had been a patient in the Jamama Hospital for more than three months, all of the staff, including myself, deeply missed his amiable and optimistic personality. I hoped that the loss I felt was like the grief described in a certain Somali proverb. "Sorrow," it says, "is like rice in the store; if a basketful is removed everyday, it will come to an end at last." Perhaps the removing of rice in that saying suggests the healing power of a daily work routine. Though each work day in Jamama was full of its own challenges and surprises, there existed a certain rhythmic pattern that seldom varied and that began with the early morning prayer of the muezzin.

One December Day

It was still dark at five a.m. when I heard the clear, echoing cry of the muezzin calling the faithful to the first prayer of the day: "Allah is good, Allah is great. Awake and pray! Allah is great, Allah is good!" At first, I noticed that call every morning, but, later, I sometimes slept through it, especially if I'd been to the hospital in the middle of the night.

By six o'clock the first signs of light streaked the sky. I didn't need an alarm because I heard the commotion of the village awakening, just beyond the compound fence. The donkeys were the first to make themselves heard. Their braying must be one of the most irritating sounds I've ever heard. During our first few weeks in Jamama, Mary threatened that donkey closest to our bedroom window, but now she could sleep right through this cacophony. Soon I could hear babies crying and people shouting to each other. Our two pet monkeys outside started chattering, and I knew it was time to get up and feed them half a banana before they'd leap onto our tin roof.

Eventually I had become accustomed to cold showers since there was no water heater. When the generator was running in the evenings, a pump drew water from the well to a holding tank about fifteen feet in the air. So gravity supplied water for our use. In the mornings, the water was cold and fresh, but sometimes by late afternoon the sun had warmed the tank, making the water almost comfortable for a shower. Still, I preferred to take a brisk morning shower and then eat a breakfast of Mary's homemade granola with a banana and milk.

On my short walk to the hospital at seven, I noticed a few women on the other side of the fence, balancing jugs of river water on their heads. The December grass was so dry it crackled under my feet and smelled a bit like the burnt straw and hay I remembered when my parents' barn burned down in a lightning storm. As I neared the hospital, I could smell the charcoal fire where families of patients cooked their breakfast. In a few days it would be the first day of winter in Indiana, but here it was just another day in the dry season. I wondered if there was snow back home and how the doctors were getting along. The last letter from the Medical Center in Markle informed us that flu had hit the area hard and that they missed us.

In the hospital I noticed that Martha had delivered a baby during the night. In the past, I would have first checked on Hussein and we would have spent time visiting. Now that he had died, I felt a pang of grief each morning as I passed by his room.

In the men's ward I checked on a cataract patient whose surgery had been completed the day before. We had decided that I would perform one cataract surgery every Wednesday. This man was recovering well without pain, and I felt like removing the patch to check his eye, but the book stated not to remove it and the eye protector for at least forty-eight hours.

Another patient in the men's ward that morning was a fourteen-year-old whose lymph nodes in his neck were unusually swollen. I admitted him several days earlier when he arrived from the bush with a caravan of nomads. He was running a high fever, and, though the nomads were moving on, an older brother had stayed to cook for him.

In the States, I would have first suspected a lymphoma (cancer of the lymph tissue), but here the most likely diagnosis was scrofula (tuberculosis of the lymph glands). Had it been cancer, I could have offered no treatment, but, since it was tuberculosis, his prognosis was good, if he continued his medication. We administered daily Streptomycin injections as well as pills of INH (Isoniazid) and PAS (para-amino-salicylic acid). That morning, I could tell for the first time that the nodes were softer, a little smaller, and that the fever had broken. Many times scrofula is caused by drinking milk from cattle or camels with tuberculosis, so, at home, we carefully boiled all of the milk we bought.

Several of the patients I saw next were receiving intravenous fluids as they were admitted with severe diarrhea and dehydration from cholera. At the hospital, we prepared all our own IV fluids since there were none available to purchase.

I had almost finished my rounds in the men's ward when Pauline rushed in. "Come with me to the women's ward," she said. "There's something I think you'll want to see." There, in a bed, was an eight-year-old girl we had admitted the day before with anemia and a large swollen abdomen. Now her bed was covered with several hundred crawling, squirming round worms (ascariasis). One even crawled from her nose, and she had just coughed up several others. The bed itself wriggled with others expelled from her rectum. They ranged from two to six inches in length and were light tan in color.

We had given her a de-worming medicine when we admitted her to the hospital as we did for almost all of the children and for some of the adults. Usually when we gave this medicine to others we would notice a few worms, but nothing like this. I had seen round worms in the States when a mother might frantically show one in a glass jar that her child had passed. This Somali girl would now have the opportunity to gain nourishment from her food and would be on the path to better health.

I finished rounds by visiting the separate isolation rooms away from the hospital. Two men, both recently admitted with active pulmonary tuberculosis, were too weak to make the trip to the hospital every day for an injection. They were from the bush, and a family member stayed with them to prepare their meals.

One thing we could almost always offer patients as a supplement to the meals family members fixed was powdered milk. Mennonite Central Committee (MCC) sent us cartons of bagged milk from the Netherlands. We used this in the hospital and sometimes sent it home with sick children who had no other way of getting milk. Most of the nomads could drink camel milk even in the dry season, but in villages like Jamama it was a rare commodity.

My interpreter for the week was Fatama, a second-year nursing student who was very intelligent but exceptionally quiet. I needed her assistance as a translator, and she also gained knowledge from our consultations with patients about their diseases. The first patients waiting for me in the clinic were ones we had seen Wednesday who had now returned with results from their lab tests. We could study sputum for Tuberculosis bacillus and stool and urine for parasites. Blood gave us data on sugar diabetes, malaria, kidney and liver function, and for a complete blood count. Some patients would receive their lab results the same day they saw us, but others had to come back the next day.

I spent the first hour in the clinic telling patients about the diseases we had diagnosed and the needed treatments. One man had arrived the day before with blood in his urine and painful urination. In the States, we would have suspected cancer of the bladder or kidney or, perhaps, a kidney stone. But here along the Juba River, where people waded in canals infested with the parasite Schistosoma haematobium, they would exhibit dilation of the veins, especially of the cystic vein, which produces irritability of the bladder and thereby bleeding and pain. This disease, called schistosomiasis or bilharziosis, was endemic in our area. We started this patient on injections the day before, and the report on his urine came back positive. He would receive ten days of injections, and Fatama explained to him how he could prevent the disease in the future by not wading in stagnant water or by wearing boots.

I was eager for ten o'clock to arrive because that was when the laundry woman brought me a cup of *shai*. I drank mine straight, but most of the Somali employees added milk. This was hot tea on a hot day, but its spicy sweetness quenched my thirst and gave me the energy I needed until lunch.

During the second part of the morning, I was glad to have a female nursing student with me because several of the patients I treated then were women with vaginal bleeding or severe pelvic pain. My screener, Hussein, could not perform a pelvic examination because he was a Muslim male, but, because I was an infidel, I could, as long as I was accompanied by a female nurse. Fatama explained the procedure, as most of the women had never had a pelvic exam before.

One woman had a large mass in her vagina that originated from the cervix. It was hard and fastened to the sides of the vagina. She told us she had experienced pain and bleeding for over two years. I was convinced that she had cervical cancer, but, without a pathologist in the entire country, we could not get a pathological diagnosis. We informed this woman she had a disease for which there was no cure, but that we could give her medicine to help relieve the pain. I felt sorry for her, but there was nothing I could do. The Somali nurses always wanted me to tell everyone that I could cure them, but I stressed the need to be honest with the patients if we wanted them to believe in us and respect us.

We didn't finish the morning clinic until about twelve-thirty, so, after checking the hospital, I walked home for lunch with the whole family now that our daughters, Marlis and Shari, were home for winter break. Mary said that Chester had stopped by the post office, but the mail hadn't arrived. Marlis had spent part of the morning mixing a batch of refrigerator ice cream while Shari cleaned out the shells we had gathered from our last trip to the ocean.

Stephen told me during lunch how Charley, his ostrich, had darted out of his hands: "He ran so fast that Eric and I couldn't catch him. He ran right through a hole in the fence and was gone. We could always catch him before." I explained that Charley had grown large enough and fast enough to fend for himself in the wild, so it was okay that he was free.

After lunch, we lay down for short naps. I got up a little early to organize the material for my three o'clock nursing class on pneumonia. These classes were always enjoyable because the students were so eager to learn; they would sit attentively, taking notes and asking pertinent questions. Since we didn't have any textbooks, Mary typed the material I prepared for handouts.

At four, I returned to the hospital because Hussein had scheduled two patients for tooth extractions. There were no dentists in the country, so on their vacations, mission workers traveled to Nairobi to see a dentist for check ups or fillings. Both Somali patients had painful, infected molars, and I wished I had received some dental training in the States. The first man's tooth pulled easily with just a local anesthetic. The other man's was more painful, and I could not seem to sufficiently numb it, so I had Martha administer Ipital intravenously to sedate him for three to five minutes, just enough time to pull the tooth.

From the surgery room, I could hear cheering at the community soccer field. After finishing the extractions and making rounds again, I crossed the road to watch the game. The mission school was playing a team of teenagers from the village. Today a larger crowd than usual stood next to the stick-and-wire fence erected to keep goats and cattle out of the field. It was hard to know which team the fans were rooting for, as they seemed to cheer any good play. Today the game was close with each team having scored one goal.

Soccer was the only competitive sport I saw played in Somalia. We had a volleyball and basketball court on the mission compound where we taught those sports to the school children. The students could execute all kinds of maneuvers with their feet and heads but had trouble mastering the dexterity to dribble a basketball. I remember one eighth-grade boy, Ali, who was six foot, seven inches tall. He liked playing and was getting quite good at making baskets and dribbling. Some days he would play in a skirt, but he knew how to wrap it around his legs so that it wasn't bothersome.

At five-thirty I was called back to the hospital for an emergency. A lorry had brought a sixteen-year-old girl to the hospital along with about twenty of her friends and family. She was hysterical, as were most of her friends who were crying and shouting, making it hard to ascertain just what had happened. I finally discovered that this young woman had opened her mouth wide to eat something and now could not close it. She had been this way for three hours and lived thirty miles away in Gelib.

When I examined her, I realized she had dislocated her jaw. She was frightened and agitated, so I had the nurse give her five mg. of Valium intravenously. In about three minutes she was sufficiently relaxed for me to place my thumbs inside her mouth and push the lower jaw down and forward, popping it back into place. You could see this girl's surprise and relief as she opened and closed her mouth. Her friends began laughing and dancing, and soon they were on their way home.

At a little after six, the hospital was quiet, and I felt good about the day as I started walking back to the house. I was tired, but I knew my day had been less laborious than that of most Somalis. The setting sun was turning the faded green of our house to a soft gold tinged with pink. Since we were living on the equator, the sun rose and set quickly. It was always night before we knew it.

As I read Stephen a story after supper, one from the *Child Craft Encyclopedia* about Edison inventing the light bulb, I heard the last faint prayer call of the day. Between daylight and dusk, there was often too much noise on the compound or the soccer field to hear the prayers, but, at dawn and in the evening, we almost always heard this solemn sound settling over the land.

Shari and Marlis took turns holding three-month-old Abdi and cutting small snowflakes out of typing paper to hang on the pine branch they had procured for our "Charlie Brown" Christmas tree. Mary gave me six air-form letters that had arrived in the late afternoon. I didn't feel like writing any responses just then, but maybe I would tomorrow, so the letters could go out on Sunday. There were no students coming over to study the Bible with me that evening, so I had time to prepare a short devotional for tomorrow's morning prayer meeting. Usually Chester led these Friday meetings for the mission personnel, but he had asked me to lead this week.

Our lights blinked suddenly. We knew that in five minutes Chester would turn off the generator and it would be pitch black unless we lit our kerosene lamps. But by ten o'clock we all felt tired and ready for bed. When the drone from the generator died, we'd usually sense a deep silence descending upon the compound and village. But Thursday nights were different. They were the nights before Friday's Holy Day, the nights Somalis stayed up to celebrate with drums and dancing, and I went to sleep to the circular beat of those drums.

CHAPTER TWENTY-ONE

*The arrow will not fall out of your body
however hard you may shake.*
—Somali Proverb

In my forty-one years of medical practice and five years of medical training, I have experienced many unusual or even rare situations. In the States I could consult with fellow physicians and specialists about these cases, but in Somalia I was, for the most part, on my own to deal with extraordinary and sometimes tragic situations in which I felt utterly helpless. One of the rarest and most heartrending medical incidents I have ever witnessed began Christmas Eve while our daughters were with us during their holiday break.

Around dusk, Uglo, a Somali nurse, called me at home on the mission's makeshift phone system to ask my help with a child who had been "eaten by a dog." In Somalia, people don't say someone was "bitten" by a dog but always "eaten." However, when I looked at the child's buttocks and saw the large gash the dog had torn into his flesh, I thought "eaten" was appropriate. The boy was only about six years old and was accompanied by his father and a large group of children. I cleaned the wound thoroughly, sutured what I could, packed the rest with antiseptic gauze, placed the child on an antibiotic and give him a tetanus shot. The children told me that the wild dog looked sick, but we had no treatment for rabies prophylaxis, so I let the patient go home with orders to return in two days.

That was only the beginning of the evening's events. During the next four hours, three more boys, ages three to ten years, were brought to the hospital with bites from the same dog. After the second child arrived, I drove to the village police station and asked, "Would you please capture or kill the wild, sick dog that is eating the children of Jamama?" I preferred that they catch the dog so we could observe it for signs of rabies as we would in the States. I had learned there were no pathologists in Somalia and so to search the dog's brain for "Negri bodies," which are indicative of rabies, would be impossible.

The police station was located in the center of the village and was one of the few buildings with electricity. In a dimly lit room, several men in uniform were relaxing at a table, talking to some young men of the community. They listened intently to the story I told them, but they were quick to comment, "We can't find the dog. There are too many wild dogs running around this village, and we don't know which one to catch. We really can't be bothered with a wild dog."

They also told me there were too many children who were sick or hungry, so they could not stretch their resources to help just a few. I felt what they really meant to convey was that, because these children were from poor families, they didn't really matter. After each of the next two victims arrived at the hospital, I sent a Somali hospital representative to the station to seek assistance in stopping the attacks. No help came.

The children of the village knew that I wanted the dog dead or alive. The next day, Christmas, when our family had just finished our noon meal, we heard a commotion coming from the front of the compound. What we saw next was amazing. The compound guard ushered in a large group of children, all singing and shouting as they danced toward our house. In the center of the spectacle, several boys carried a dead dog tied by its feet to a stick as if it were a goat or pig going to market. The village children had found the sick, malnourished dog and had killed it. Now they were bringing it to show me. What the police had said could not be done, these children had succeeded in doing with sticks and stones.

Even though this was the end of that dog eating any more children, it was not the end of this tragic situation. Over the next several days I talked to all the fathers of the children who had been injured and told them the severity of the situation. I was sure the children had been infected with rabies. I sent telegrams to the government's medical officials in Kismayu and Mogadishu to inquire about any rabies antibody injections available for these children. They assured me there were none in the country because Somalia was free of rabies. They also decreed that the children could not leave the country to obtain treatment. This was the government's usual approach to problems. First, they denied the problem, and then, if the problem couldn't be ignored, they admitted that they didn't have the means to handle the situation. I could not buy any serum because there seemed to be none available.

The children's wounds healed, and I lost contact with the families. I did hear that one father took his son to Mogadishu and was able to obtain four or five injections for him on the black market. Another father fled with his son over the border to Kenya and was able to find a full series of injections in Nairobi. Although I never heard what happened, I feel that this child was probably protected from rabies. The clinical disease can take up to a year to develop since it sometimes takes that long for the virus to reach the brain from the point of entry. In February, news of the first death reached me; one of the children had died at home in Jamama.

About Easter, a child was brought to the clinic with a high fever, dehydration, and a history of being sick for only a few days. He suffered from choking episodes and spasmodic catching of breath while also experiencing profuse secretions of sticky saliva that he tried to spit out. He was one of the children bitten by the dog on Christmas Eve.

Years ago we called rabies "hydrophobia" because, when coming down with the disease, patients cannot swallow and become frantic when presented with water. I asked the boy if he wanted a drink of *biyo*, the Somali word for water. He became hysterical and flung himself around. He could not swallow and offering him a drink of water was like offering to drown him. Now that he displayed the disease, there was no treatment for him anywhere in the world except to keep him comfortable.

I explained this to his father, who decided to take him home. I gave him some rectal suppositories that would make his final hours more comfortable by preventing seizures and helping him to sleep. I had an overwhelming, desperate feeling of knowing I could do nothing to save this young life. I took the father and his son home in our Fiat to his small house at the edge of Jamama, the one small thing I could do for them since the father had carried his son two miles to reach the hospital.

I never heard what happened to the other two boys since we left for home eight months after those bites. I am sure the child who went to Kenya was cured, but I do not feel as confident about the one who received only four injections.

Few physicians, particularly in the States, have had the experience of treating rabies in the past fifty years. My experience left me feeling weak and saddened as I realized how little I could do. There are always those patients who, like these children, can not be cured or even helped, and, as physicians, we can only show them that we do care deeply about their lives.

CHAPTER TWENTY-TWO

You tell one thing but he may hear another.
—Somali Proverb

Communicating with my patients in the developing countries of Somalia and Haiti often proved difficult for me, yet it is so vital, when you are a doctor, to be clearly understood. Communication could be hard even in Markle with patients who knew English and with whom I shared a culture.

For example, one day early in my Markle medical practice, a sixteen-year-old girl visited my office to see about losing weight. She was moderately overweight but by no means obese, and I supposed she was looking for some sort of diet pills although she never really asked for any. Since I seldom prescribed diet medications during my years of medical practice and certainly never any pills to teenagers, we spent a considerable amount of time discussing her dietary habits and what changes she could make to help control her weight. She needed to reduce her caloric intake, increase her exercise, and realize that weight loss is a long range goal. We talked about the changes she could make in her diet and how she might be more active.

Then I asked her, "Do you have any will power?"

She answered, "Grandma buys it once in awhile, but I really don't care for it." I felt I had lost the battle with her that day.

Another example of miscommunication occurred while I was making a house call one evening a few years back in the small town of Uniondale about three miles from our home. I was called to the house of an elderly couple where the husband had been ill with vomiting and an upset stomach for the past twenty-four hours. During the examination, the wife requested, "Don't give my husband any of those suppositories for vomiting because the last time you gave them the edges really hurt him something terrible." I found out that they had never removed the tin foil from the suppository. After that experience, I always wrote on the envelope, "Remove tinfoil before inserting rectally."

In Somalia, the language barrier was always present because I knew very little of the language and my translators were limited in the English they knew. It didn't help that the Somali language has very few medical terms and even lacks vocabulary for symptoms we commonly describe in English. Patients would often spend several minutes explaining with great emotion what was wrong. Then the translator would say nothing.

I would ask, "What did he just say?"

My nurse translator would reply, "Oh, he really isn't saying anything. He doesn't make sense."

I would insist that he tell me anyway. It was usually something related to how the patient developed his symptoms and so strange that the nurse was too embarrassed to even translate the meaning. The cause, from the viewpoint of the patient, was something that happened just before the symptoms started. It might be that the cough came on because he had stubbed his toe while bringing the goat in from the pasture six weeks before. Or he now has diarrhea and a stomachache because he cut his hair before his daughter's marriage. These facts were crucial to the patients, and they wanted to be sure I understood why they were sick. With this logic, it was difficult to teach Somali patients how to prevent illnesses and to avoid spreading tuberculosis and other contagious diseases.

One afternoon a nineteen-year-old girl was brought to the hospital with a month-old burn on her left arm. Fatama was from a poor family that lived deep in the bush, and she wore a tattered, dark red wrap-around. The story given to me was that she had seizures, and, when one occurred while cooking, she fell into the fire. Most of her burns healed, but not the one on her left forearm. When I examined it, her forearm was red and macerated, greenish pus seeped from the burn, and maggots had burrowed into the flesh. Of course she was admitted to the hospital and placed on intravenous antibiotics. Then I cleaned the area of all foreign material and trimmed away the dead tissue.

After several days, I took a skin graft from her leg and attached it to her arm. In fourteen days, the arm looked much better with no sign of infection and the skin graft had taken hold. I felt I could send her home. But Fatama looked unhappy and would not smile. So I asked her what was wrong.

"I am homesick," she said, "and I don't understand why you took the skin off my leg and gave it to the cat just because I am poor."

I realized then that I must have done an exceptionally poor job of explaining to her the concept of a skin graft.

CHAPTER
TWENTY-THREE

He who does not understand what is going on now
will not understand what is going to happen.
—Somali Proverb

Every culture includes folk medical practices passed on from one generation to the next. Some of these are harmless and some aren't. We have many such practices in the States, and some communities and families have more than others. Mary recalls her grandmother's treatment for warts: rub half of a raw potato on the wart and then throw it over your shoulder. When Mary had a side ache, she was to stop, pick up a stone, and toss it over the same shoulder as the pain. In elementary school, I remember a classmate who, whenever he had a cold, wore garlic in a cheesecloth sack around his neck to prevent asthma attacks. However, as I recollect, all it did was keep his friends at a distance.

Most of the time the greatest danger from folk remedies is that they may prevent people from seeking appropriate early treatment for a curable disease. For instance, a sixty-eight-year-old patient of mine was once brought to the emergency room with an acute stroke. His blood pressure was 250/120, he couldn't speak, and his left side was paralyzed. Since this man's blood pressure had been well controlled, I told his wife I was surprised that it was so high. She replied, "He stopped taking all his medicine thirty days ago because someone told him that garlic cured high blood pressure. I told him to continue his medicine, but he said garlic would be so much cheaper." Garlic was commonly prescribed for hypertension before 1940, but this mistake cost my patient eight years of extreme disability before he died.

An example of a particularly dangerous folk practice was one I saw in 1976, when the Markle Medical Center started a clinic with Project Help in Haiti. A number of infants came into our Haitian clinic with fever and seizures. These newborns had tetanus. It was heart-rending to watch these newborns die and to see the grief on their mothers' faces. In Haiti, where virtually all babies are delivered at home by older women serving as midwives, the traditional practice dictates that after the baby is delivered, the cord is cut, usually with a rusty, used blade, and the end of the umbilical cord is dipped in cow dung. The midwives didn't detect the connection because not every baby contracts tetanus by this procedure. Our clinic, however, was seeing about one baby a week with tetanus until we started free prenatal classes for the women and gave them a kit supplied by U.S. churches, consisting of a blanket, gown, soap, safety pins, a short piece of umbilical tape to tie the cord, and a new razor blade. Such efforts were started all over Haiti by missions and government groups. Today it is rare to see a child with infant tetanus unless that child was born in a remote mountain village.

In Somalia, there were also many practices handed down from one generation to the next, and many were dangerous to people's health. One practice, in particular, often created severe health problems. Just as Christians, when they are seriously ill, often go to a pastor for prayer or anointing, so Somali Muslims would visit their sheikh or cleric. The religious leader would read Scripture to the patient while intermittently spitting into a cup. When he finished, the patient would then drink this holy water. What made this practice unsafe was the high incidence of tuberculosis in the country. One infected religious leader could infect a whole community in a short period of time.

Another dangerous practice was one that could also prove helpful to me in making a medical diagnosis. I found that the typical Somali would first go to a bush doctor who'd burn the skin over the place where the patient felt pain to drive away the evil spirit causing the discomfort. If I examined a patient with multiple burns on his chest wall, I knew the problem was in his chest. If the burns covered the chest, it was probably a severe, deep cough. If the burns appeared on the throat and upper chest, it was usually hoarseness with a bronchial cough. If there were many burns with a number of very old scars, I knew the disease had been present for a long time. Burns on the lower back might indicate arthritis of the back or just back strain, but if burns also extended down the back of one leg, I might also suspect the patient had lumbar disc disease with sciatica or shingles (herpes zoster). Burn marks might be present over the liver, kidneys, or even the face. Many times the burns would be infected which would only add to the illness.

It especially bothered me to see babies and small children with burns because I knew the process must have needlessly hurt them. Sometimes, instead of burning, the bush doctors used a sharp blade and cut the skin multiple times to let the "bad blood" out, a procedure reminiscent of the European and American practice of "bleeding" patients.

Folk practices like burning and bleeding continue for centuries because they usually seem to work. Our bodies are so wondrously made that most of the time they simply heal themselves. So whatever we do, when the pain ceases, we think we know the magical cure.

It was only when a Somali did not get better after the "holy water," the burns, and the cuts that he or she would make the trip to the mission hospital. As a result, patients coming to see us were usually quite ill. This was especially true for those with tuberculosis, the number one killer among chronic diseases in our part of Africa. The typical tuberculosis patient was gaunt, with reduced muscle mass. His pale face would appear emaciated, with sunken cheeks. In his labored breaths, I'd hear a constant rattle, and his sputum would often be streaked with blood. He would be shivering, with his head covered even on hot days. Some patients would exhibit open, draining sores on their necks, arm pits, or groins. They would usually be accompanied by a family member who assisted them into the clinic.

Our hospital was one of the few places in the country where a chest x-ray was available. Usually we would just do fluoroscopy, a process that allowed me to look directly at the chest but without a film for comparison at a later time. I'd perform all of the fluoroscopies and take all of the x-rays at the same time each day because these processes required electricity from the generator.

We could also administer sputum tests for the tuberculosis bacillus, and if the diagnosis was tuberculosis, we had procured medicine from UNICEF and other sources with which to treat the patient. This medicine was effective and inexpensive. We found no drug resistance because we seldom found patients who had received any prior treatment. Initially, we saw tuberculosis patients daily, so we could give them streptomycin injections, as well as their oral medicine, and advise them about their disease. The patients would recover, and we would simply lose track of many of them as they returned to the bush with a three-month supply of medicine. Some would return for more medicine but others would not. If the patient lived in Jamama, however, our Somali health nurses could follow up on their treatment. We stressed the continuation of medicine for one year after the cessation of symptoms and a negative sputum.

My most unusual encounter with folk medicine began one morning when a very thin teenage girl came to see me, accompanied by her father. She looked malnourished and dehydrated, and the story her father told was tragic. After his daughter had developed a toothache in a left, lower molar, she had gone to a bush doctor who burned an area on the outside and inside of her cheek over the painful tooth. When the skin and flesh sloughed off, a hole appeared in her lower cheek. She would put food and liquids in her mouth, but they would escape through the hole. The burned area and hole then became infected, and the infection extended up her jaw to the tempomandibular joint which kept her from opening and closing her mouth. As a result, she could not speak, nor could she open her mouth to chew. Whatever liquids she took ran through the hole in her cheek, and, still, she had the toothache.

We of course started intravenous fluids, antibiotics, and vitamins. The nurses found ways to get the highest protein drinks we could make down into her stomach, and I pulled the infected tooth through the hole in her cheek. We started her on heat packs and applied physical therapy to the jaw to help it gain movement. In four weeks, she was healthy enough for me to repair the defect in her cheek. Eventually seeing this pretty eighteen-year-old girl and her father smile was reward enough for our efforts.

Chapter Twenty-Four

The man whom you failed to know within an
hour you will not know within a year.
—Somali Proverb

Soon after Christmas, while our daughters were still home on winter break, a well-dressed, middle-aged Russian doctor from Kismayu and his interpreter arrived at the hospital. Since the Russian physicians in Kismayu specialized in only one area of medicine and were poorly trained to treat tropical illnesses, we allowed them to bring their families to the clinic on Thursday afternoons. But this wasn't a Thursday, and I had never seen this physician before.

Soon after meeting me, he asked to see "Mr. Hassen's records." We retrieved the file, and he spent several hours poring over the contents. Our records included the vital information but nothing as complete as in the States. However, with a hospitalization of over three months, Hussein's records comprised our thickest file. The Russian doctor informed me he had been asked by the court system to review the hospital records and to exhume the patient's body for an autopsy. When he left, he told me he would contact me later with his findings.

One week later, the prosecuting attorney from Kismayu arrived at our hospital, asking to see my credentials. I showed him my letter from the Somali Ministry of Health recognizing me as a physician and giving me license to be in the country. However, he was not satisfied and wanted more proof. Mary and I searched the house until we found a copy of my diploma from Indiana University School of Medicine, a copy of my Indiana License to practice medicine, and a letter from Paul Bender, the administrator of Wells Community Hospital, indicating that I had privileges there and was in good standing. I sensed a rather cold response from the attorney, but he seemed satisfied and left the hospital. He never mentioned why he wanted this verification.

Life quickly returned to its usual routine of caring for tuberculosis patients, treating snakebites, performing surgeries, and handling complicated pregnancies and deliveries. The weather during January and February was extremely hot, and since it had been nine to ten months without any rainfall, many people were facing starvation, especially the poorest and most ill.

Chapter Twenty-Five

These youth taught their mother to give birth.
—Somali Proverb

Over the years, one of the most enjoyable and exciting parts of my family practice has been obstetrics. But it could also be stressful since deliveries do not usually come at the most convenient times. Babies often arrived in the middle of the night, when the office was the busiest, or when I was ready to depart with my family for a special occasion. The deliveries I performed in Africa were often less than cheerful events because usually only the complicated ones were performed at our hospital.

In the 1960s and 1970s more than ninety percent of my deliveries in the States occurred with married women who, with their husbands, were excitedly looking forward to the birth of their baby. By the 1990s, that percentage had changed. Thirty to forty percent of the pregnancies involved unwed girls, and expectations were not always happy. However, to hold a squirming newborn as she takes her first breath, wrinkles her face, and gives out a healthy cry always makes one feel awed at the miracle of birth.

Once I received a call at two in the morning from a mother of eleven children. She asked if I would see her oldest child, a seventeen-year-old daughter, who was suffering from severe stomach pains. The mother said that this daughter seldom complained of anything but now was very uncomfortable. During the early years of my practice, we did not have a staffed emergency room, and, when someone called at night with a medical concern, it was easier to either make a house call or have the person come directly to the office. If I merely gave advice over the phone, I would lie awake waiting for the phone to ring again or wondering if I had made the right diagnosis and if the patient was getting along okay. I therefore made some unnecessary visits but gained peace of mind knowing I had started appropriate treatment. So I told the mother to bring her daughter to the office immediately, and I would be there to see her.

When I watched the girl walk into the room and climb onto the table, I was already pretty sure of the diagnosis. As I felt her stomach, I immediately knew she was pregnant, and when I examined her vaginally it was quite clear that the head was already crowning. With one uterine contraction, the young woman delivered a seven-pound girl. I asked the grandmother if she had not wondered if her daughter was pregnant, and she replied, "I thought she was only putting on a little weight." The new mother's response was the smile across her face. I was glad I took the stomachache seriously.

Over the course of my practice, I delivered close to one thousand babies. One I even delivered from the restroom stool in our hospital emergency room. As I was completing paperwork, I glimpsed a young woman streaking past me to the restroom. Next I heard a scream. Rushing in, I rescued the full-term infant male from the water of the commode, clamped the cord, and listened to the welcomed cry. This gave a new meaning to the concept of "hydrotherapy" for the delivery of babies.

In the '60s and '70s it was helpful that my partner, Dr. LeRoy Kinzer, and I could do caesarean sections. Whether you are a doctor in a rural Indiana community with a hospital staffed only by family practitioners or the only doctor in a developing world hospital such as the one in Jamama, it is important to be able to perform this surgical procedure. At Bluffton, most C-sections could be performed during the hospital's morning surgery schedule, but others required immediate action—as I experienced most dramatically one time when a woman's uterus ruptured during labor. By immediately pulling together a surgical team, we were able to deliver a live baby from the mother's abdominal cavity and save the mother's life.

In Somalia, though, over ninety-nine percent of all children were delivered at home without a physician present. Most were attended to by some older woman in the household or by a woman serving as a midwife but without any formal training. It was fairly common to ask a woman the number of children she had and find out that she only had one surviving child but eight or ten previous pregnancies. Many infants died at birth and some in the first few years of life. I saw only those women who had severe problems with labor and delivery, some deciding to come in only after many days in labor. Often the mothers would be ill and the baby dead.

The nurses performed the uncomplicated deliveries. The mothers who came to the hospital for these were often from families with a close relationship to the hospital, or their husbands were wealthy owners of banana plantations or held important positions in the community. A few women even came to the clinic for prenatal appointments and then for the delivery. But most chose not to come or could not because they lived far away in the bush or desert.

These women wanted children more than anything else in life. If a woman arrived with a dead fetus still inside her, I tried everything I could to avoid performing a C-section. Most likely, with the next pregnancy, the woman would not be visiting a hospital and the risk of a ruptured uterus during labor or some other complication would be much greater with a previous C-section. Some women traveled to the hospital with an infant's arm or leg hanging out, the appendage often gangrenous and swollen. Many of these women suffered dehydration and were running a fever. A vacuum extractor, an instrument that can be attached to the infant's scalp in the birth canal, eliminated some of the need for forceps and worked especially well with babies who had been dead for several days. These were not in use in the United States of the early 1970s but were frequently used in England and France with success. We always worked hard to save the mother's life, especially since we knew so many other lives depended on her.

One evening a woman arrived at the hospital for what appeared to be the routine delivery of her fourth child. Her husband, Akim, farmed a banana plantation along the Juba River outside of Jamama, but they lived in the village. A Muslim man may marry up to four wives, and this was Akim's oldest wife, a woman close to forty. One of the missionary nurses delivered her baby boy, and both baby and mother were recovering well so they were taken to a room that evening. The husband wanted a private room because an older aunt, a woman in her sixties, was going to stay with his wife and care for her overnight. During the night, the patient experienced increasingly heavy uterine bleeding, but this bleeding was not brought to the nurse's attention until she made rounds and found the room covered with blood and the patient in shock, gasping for breath. I was called, and, even though we worked for several hours to save her, she died.

The aunt said she had jumped on her niece's stomach to stop the bleeding and had given her herbs. How difficult it was for all of us to have a maternal death in our hospital and to realize that it should not have occurred. We realized too late that we needed to be careful about whom we permitted to stay with a patient. Had the mother been by herself in a room or with a roommate, there would have been a call for help and we would have been able to provide immediate and appropriate care.

The newborn boy was healthy, but now he had no mother to care for and nurse him. The father, realizing the danger of his son's situation, wanted him to stay in the hospital for six months to a year. In Somalia, as in many developing world countries, a child who is not nursed with breast milk will not survive. Two babies were brought to our clinic whose mothers had died at home in childbirth. In both cases, we were able to find a family member who had not breast-fed for several years but whose breast milk came in and so was able to nurse. These babies survived with surrogate mothers, but for Akim's child, no appropriate woman willing to try to nurse him could be found, and we knew the hospital was no place for a healthy newborn. So Mary and I decided to bring the baby into our house as a part of our family for awhile.

Akim was excited about this development and gave his whole-hearted support. Some of the women in his household, however, were not as supportive. But as the family, visiting weekly, saw the child's good health and the rate at which he grew on the milk and food that Mary provided, they gradually gave their support. Akim wanted us to name his son, but we insisted that he give him a name appropriate for his family. He named him Abdi. We raised Abdi Akim the first ten months of his life, until we were ready to return to the States.

CHAPTER TWENTY-SIX

It is bad with women and it is bad without them.
—Somali Proverb

I have been describing what it was like to have been a medical missionary in the poorest of African nations—but mostly from a physician's point of view. Being a housewife and mother in Somalia was also a challenge for Mary. Because we had so little time to investigate what it would be like to live in Africa before we agreed to go, Mary, in fact, did not think it wise to go. We would be pulling our children out of school and interrupting our lives for a year. We would also have a very short time to prepare. Stephen, however, who was four, had expressed his desire to go, as had his sister, Marlis, who would be entering fourth grade. They envisioned the adventure of seeing African animals and viewed the trip as one long safari.

During this time of decision-making, Mary and I were sitting around the kitchen table one evening when Shari, our oldest daughter, walked into the room. She would be an eighth grader and, since we didn't know yet how she felt about going, we decided to let her cast the deciding vote.

"Let's go," she said without hesitation. And with all three children onboard to go, Mary reluctantly agreed.

Preparation for our departure to Somalia, if only for one year, was a daunting task, and it fell primarily upon Mary's shoulders. She had to find a house-sitter, and she also had to decide what to take. We could not send trunks or boxes by oversea carrier, since it would take them so long they would arrive six months after we did. That meant packing one suitcase for each of us and carrying on as much weight as we were allowed.

Being transplanted from Markle to Jamama wasn't easy for any of us, either, but Mary found it more difficult. She suffered more from the heat. Whereas the rest of us would sweat when we were hot, she would only get over-heated and red. The following is a composite description of Mary's typical day, made up from letters she composed to her parents after several months in Somalia.

Dear Mom and Dad,

Greetings from hot, dry Somalia. In this letter I shall try to tell you about our daily routine of living here in Jamama. At about five a.m. we are awakened by the village sheikh calling Muslims to the first prayer of the day. We fall back asleep and wake up again at about 6:30 to the noise of roosters crowing and villagers starting their day.

Gerald is usually at the hospital by seven o'clock, and Hawa, the maid, comes at the same time. If she is feeling well, she greets me with a big smile. If her face is covered by her scarf with only her sad eyes showing, then I know she doesn't feel well. Hawa doesn't speak English, and I don't speak Somali, so we communicate by playing charades. The family has already had breakfast by this time so, while I care for Abdi, she starts clearing the table. Then she makes the charcoal fire for cooking, boils drinking water, sweeps the sand that the wind blows in daily, and, on bread-making day, stirs up the ingredients for a couple of loaves.

From ten o'clock until eleven, Hawa walks home to breast-feed her baby. When she comes back, she puts the bread dough in the oven, and we soon start to prepare dinner. This is our big meal of the day, and it consists of meat sauce over rice or pasta. Occasionally, we have an eggplant soufflé, a casserole when potatoes are available or barbeque sandwiches. Almost always, we have some kind of fresh fruit. Sometimes I make ice cream in the freezer compartment of the refrigerator. A salad is out of the question because leafy green vegetables just aren't available.

Hawa's work is finished for the day at around two o'-clock when the dishes are washed and the kitchen is clean. From two to three is rest time for everyone in the compound, including Gerald and the nurses. Gerald goes back to the hospital at three, and the typing lessons I teach start at four with the last student going home at six-thirty. We usually eat our evening meal of leftovers by seven or when Gerald gets done at the hospital. Omar, a teenage school boy, arrives at about six-thirty. He dusts, polishes shoes, irons, does the evening dishes, etc. Omar can speak English and likes to read to Stephen because the books for a four-year-old are in easy English, only he reads so slowly that it usually puts Stephen to sleep. Omar is probably about seventeen years old and is in the eighth grade here at the Juba School. He is a very kind, considerate boy and is constantly asking questions about the U.S. When we arrived here, I told the missionaries that it wasn't necessary for us to have house help, but they informed me that the last family had hired Hawa and Omar and we needed to keep supporting them. So now I have a clear conscience about having hired house help!

The only time of the day that we regularly have electricity is from six until ten in the evenings, but on Tuesday and Friday mornings the generator is turned on so that we can do laundry and the hospital can perform surgeries. We have a wringer-type washer, and we hang clothes on the line outside where the sun is so hot and the wind is so strong that clothes dry quickly. In fact, it's so windy that clothes are often wound around the line several times when I take them down.

As for shopping, Catherine and I walk to the shops as the village borders the compound. Walking in the town, we have to be careful to step over the little dug out trenches which serve as the septic system. We usually take our boys along, and this draws a parade of children, laughing and calling us infidels, throwing small stones and dried cow dung. It is common for some of the more adventurous children to quickly feel our hair and skin. Stephen, since he is blond with blue eyes, gets the most attention, and when he turns red in the face from embarrassment, this intrigues the children further.

The small shops are hot and airless—and I can't take being in them for long. Items are stored on shelves behind a counter, and you tell the owner what you want, or, since I don't know the language, I point my finger at the product. Sometimes, if the shopkeepers can't understand us, they let us come behind the counter to get what we want.

We can buy a few canned foods such as string beans, tomato paste, pears, and apricots. The canned fruits are mushy, though, and taste bland so we eat mainly fresh fruits. Raisins are terribly expensive. I buy them from open, uncovered, fly-and-bug-infested boxes, and so when I get home I have more than raisins. I wash them and put them in the oven at a low temperature for about twenty minutes to sterilize them. I can buy plenty of rice, spaghetti, and sometimes eggplants and white or sweet potatoes. We always have a following of children and some adults while shopping. After all, we have a lot of money. We can buy a whole can of tomato paste while the village people can afford only a spoonful on a piece of paper to take home for their meat sauce. Since they do not have any refrigerators, they buy only what they can use at each meal.

I might add that the flour is so buggy that I must sift it every time I want to use some. When I first got here, I sifted a Tupperware container of flour so I wouldn't have to get the sifter out every time I needed some flour. Later, when I went to use some, I couldn't believe my eyes—the flour looked like it was moving. Now I sift the flour just before I use any. Chester keeps a huge burlap sack of sugar on his screened porch for our use. This is not refined white sugar but the brown, raw kind, and I might add that the ants love to get into it. Perhaps these bugs and ants help supply our diet with protein.

If we want to buy bananas, mangoes, papaya, meat, sugar cane, etc., we go to the outdoor market. The village people only butcher once a week, and the meat is hung outdoors where they just cut off a piece for you. I always send Hawa for the meat because I know my eyes, nose, and stomach couldn't handle it, let alone eat it afterward! Sometimes she brings home a piece of meat that she calls a fillet. This meat we can cook like a roast, only it takes all day and still is tough to chew. We mainly grind it up for meat sauce or barbeques.

One day the meat was scarce, and Hawa brought home something that looked like a porcupine. I told her she could take it home as it didn't look like anything we could eat. We think it was a cow's stomach, and she seemed glad to take it home. We are told that when the dry season comes and meat becomes scarce, the Somalis will butcher their camels, but they don't kill them unless they are sick or too old to work. The meat is so tough because the animals haven't any fat. I tried to make meatloaf one day, but it wouldn't stick together.

Since our refrigerator uses kerosene, I send Omar to buy the fuel, which comes in two gallon metal cans. I always buy five cans because the refrigerator really drinks it up. Omar buys it and then hires a man with his donkey to carry it to the house for one shilling and fifty, about twenty cents in our money.

The village people bring milk to the door for us to buy, and then each household needs to pasteurize it. Eggs are also sold at the door, and I was told to put the eggs in water and, if they float, I shouldn't buy them. Our house is the closest one to the village, and when I first arrived, I bought every egg that came to the door and tested them later until the other missionaries started complaining that they weren't getting any eggs. Since the weather is so hot and the chickens lay their eggs outside in the sun, it doesn't take long for them to rot. One day I boiled some and must have been careless in testing because one exploded all over me.

Villagers covet our empty tin cans. We have trouble keeping a tin can with food in it for our monkeys. Each time we go out to the back stoop to feed them, the can is gone. The hospital also uses our clean cans as containers to dispense medicine. I help the nurses fold paper containers for the pills patients take home.

Baby Abdi continues to grow like a healthy baby should. Almost every time Somalis comes to see him, they ask if I give him medicine and what does he eat. When I tell them I only give him straight cow's milk and no medicine, they are amazed and I don't know if they really believe me. Somali babies wear copper and leather bands around their arms and legs. We think the copper is jewelry, and the leather bands have a pouch with words from the Qur'an inside to protect them. At times, mothers put a mixture of blood and manure on their babies' scalps to keep them from getting sick.

The Somalis don't use diapers, and when Abdi's grandmother comes to hold him, she keeps fingering the safety pins that hold the cloth diaper on (no throwaways here!). I imagine that those metal things have her puzzled. One time when she came, Abdi was sleeping on his stomach and she had a fit. I soon found out that Somalis only let their babies sleep on their backs. In fact, no Somali sleeps on his or her stomach—child or adult.

It is so wonderful having Shari and Marlis here for Christmas vacation. How we miss them when they are in school. Last Saturday Catherine and I took our children swimming and shell hunting at the Indian Ocean near Kismayu. The tide was out and we walked about half a mile out on the ocean bed and ate a picnic lunch of zamboozies. These consist of fried hamburger, peppers, onions, and garlic stuffed into a pocket of dough and then deep-fat fried. They are delicious, but we eat bananas with them because they have some kind of hot sauce added that burns all the way down. On the way home, we got stuck in the sand four times. We all got out and pushed which wasn't fun with our feet in hot sand and the sun beating down on our backs.

Sunday night a nurse at the hospital called to say he had just killed a poisonous snake that had crawled into the nursing station and nearly bit him. We went to see it and were struck by how small it was. It may have been a mamba since those extremely poisonous snakes are very thin. I came home and searched for places where a mamba could enter underneath our front or back door. I took a scatter rug and stuffed it into the space between the door and floor on the back porch. I don't have another rug for the front door so I'm hoping that there is enough traffic in the front to discourage any creepy crawler from coming in. That night got all the missionaries talking about the snakes they have found in their houses.

We have killed three scorpions on the floor since we arrived. They have a terribly painful sting and can be fatal to certain people. I detest pulling out the kitchen drawer where I keep my linens. Every time I open the drawer several huge cockroaches scurry out, and they are at least this long _____.
Hawa was sweeping Stephen's room yesterday when all of a sudden she yelled for me to come. When I got there, she pointed under Stephen's bed and shouted, "Snake!" I got brave and looked, but it was only Stephen's black leather belt. What a scare. So far, no snakes in this house and it better stay that way.

Mom, in your last letter you asked if we have a lot of Lemon Pledge for all the dust in our house. We could go broke buying it, but, of course, it isn't available to tempt us. I can wash the dust off the furniture with a wet rag everyday and get several buckets of dirty water.

We haven't received any mail from the States for three weeks. This mail system is for the birds. In fact, I think birds would be faster. Maybe I should train a few carrier pigeons. We enjoy your weekly letters even if they do come late so keep them coming.

Love,
Mary

CHAPTER
TWENTY-SEVEN

It is you who need advice, it does not need you.
Somali Proverb

One of the first surgeries I performed at Jamama was the repair of a rectal fistula on a man. When I took him to surgery, I told him I was going to administer a spinal anesthetic and that he would need to lie on his stomach for the surgery. He became very apprehensive and restless. I told him he would be okay, that the surgery would fix his problem. He said, "I am not worried about the surgery. I am afraid that I might fall asleep on my stomach and die." From talking with the nurses, I discovered that Somali infants are never put to sleep on their stomachs, and so they grow-up to feel uncomfortable in that position, as if it is cutting off their breath.

When we brought baby Abdi to our house after his mother died, we placed him on his stomach to sleep. If he was fussy between feedings, we could give him a pacifier, place him on his stomach and soon, with a few pats on the back, he would be asleep. However, when his aunts came to visit and found him on his stomach, they would immediately turn him over while rapidly talking and clicking their tongues. Of course, this would awaken Abdi and he would start crying. As Abdi grew older, he learned to turn over by himself so that he could sleep comfortably on his stomach. Mary and I said he would grow up to be the only Somali who slept in that position.

A year or two after we returned to the States, a medical alert was issued to all physicians and parents: "Do not let your infants sleep on their stomach as this is related to sudden infant death syndrome (SIDS)." A study performed with thousands of infants proved what the Somalis had known for centuries.

Breast-feeding is another area in which we can learn from the Somalis. In the States, I always encouraged mothers to breast-feed their babies. I felt it was more natural, less expensive, helped with bonding and gave the infant a good nutritious start as well as immunity to disease. However, most years I would receive less than a fifty percent response. Mothers might start breast-feeding at the hospital but then would stop by the third-week return visit. They would say, "My baby didn't seem satisfied," or "My milk just would not come in." Another reason I heard was, "My mother said she could never nurse so she didn't think I would be able to either." But in Somalia all mothers were able to breast-feed their babies. Most would nurse for eighteen to twenty-four months. The babies would have grown a good many teeth before the mothers stopped.

The most difficult situation related to breast-feeding I encountered was what to do for a baby when the mother died after childbirth. Most frequently, a sister or aunt who was still breast-feeding would offer to nurse the infant. This usually worked well, but sometimes no nursing relative could be found, and the baby started out on goat, camel, or cow's milk. In these cases, the babies usually became sick and died.

Before I left the States for Somalia, Ann Landers penned a column in our newspaper in which she responded to a reader's question: "Can a woman who did not deliver a baby and so is not already nursing successfully breast-feed a newborn?" Her answer was that doctors assured her it would be impossible.

In Somalia, however, I heard several stories that contradicted this belief. In fact, on two occasions Martha was able to find an older family member who wasn't already nursing to breast-feed a newborn. Once it was an aunt who had not nursed a baby for two years.

Over the years I have learned many things from my patients if I just take the time to listen. One day at the clinic in Haiti, a woman in her fifties told me she had a sugar problem. I was skeptical since diabetes is not a major problem in developing world countries, but I asked, "How do you know that you have this problem? Did a doctor tell you this?"

She quickly replied, "Oh, no, I have not been to a doctor. I came here to tell you so I could get treatment. When I tasted my urine, it was sweet. I had three of my friends taste it, too, and two out of the three also agreed it tasted sweet."

When the lab checked her blood sugar, it was over 400 mg%. Yes, she was diabetic just as she had assured me.

CHAPTER
TWENTY-EIGHT

An old wound will not go away.
—Somali Proverb

So much of our experience in the health care field deals with sadness. We see people who are hurting, afraid, have lost loved ones, and are depressed. Sometimes we take care of patients with diseases for which there are no cures. In the Somali language there is no word for "cancer," and I found it difficult to tell patients they had a disease for which there was no cure, though telling them this usually satisfied them. Ironically, some of the most tragic cases I cared for in Somalia concerned people with disabilities that could have been prevented

Somali women who have suffered through the complications of childbirth are one such group. These women often give birth to their first baby while in their early teens. Their pelvis is small and there's no professional help at the time of delivery. Some women suffer vaginal tears that extend from the base of the urethra to the rectum and never have them repaired because no one is available to sew the laceration.

In the States these tears occasionally happen with a precipitous home delivery or a difficult instrument delivery, but doctors are trained to recognize them and to repair the laceration before the mother leaves the delivery room. Somali women are left with a fistula, or hole, from their rectum to their urethra and are incontinent of stool or urine or both. They might not be able to control their stool or urine or it might seep through their vagina. They then face problems with cleanliness and offensive odors, and their husbands turn away from them. I saw several women with deliveries in which the babies' heads were so low in the birth canal for such a long time that the pressure on the urethra caused a fistula between the urethra and vagina. Frequently these babies would be born dead or die soon after birth, and the women would continually leak urine through their vagina.

Some women did not seek medical help because they did not know it was available, and others may have just been too poor. Some may have felt such complications were simply one of the burdens of being a woman. Somali women would never allow a pelvic exam by a male Muslim physician, but because I was an infidel, it was acceptable for me to check them. Usually there would be some infection to address before I could carry out the surgical repair. Many women would also require vitamins and iron to give the healing process a boost. I found this an especially rewarding surgery to perform because it would give these women back their lives. They were always appreciative of the care we gave them, and their husbands or mothers who came to the hospital with them would also express their appreciation. I worried, though, about what would happen with their next birthing experience, and I'd tell these women to go to a hospital if at all possible.

I had been at Jamama for only a couple weeks when a seven-year-old boy was brought to me by one of the Somali nurse screeners. He said, "This boy has a hole in his urethra and so urine sprays out when he urinates."

"How did he get such a fistula?" I asked. "Was he born with it?"

"This child was circumcised by the sheikh when he was five years old," the nurse explained. "There was no anesthetic given, and the boy would not hold still. Because he thrashed around so much, the sheikh accidentally cut the urethra and now he must squat like a girl to urinate; otherwise, the urine leaks back on him and down his leg. His father would like you to help him."

I repaired the lesion as I did several others that year. Again, it would have been so much better to have prevented the problem in the first place. These boys were usually very afraid when brought to the hospital by their fathers, but they were old enough to cooperate with the surgery and post-op care.

I often think about those Somali women and boys and wonder if they are receiving any medical care now in Somalia. I recently heard of a humanitarian-run fistula hospital in Ethiopia. It is treating many women, and I wonder if women in Somalia can cross the border to obtain medical and surgical care at that hospital, even though the countries have long been enemies.

CHAPTER TWENTY-NINE

The absence of knowledge is the absence of light.
—Somali Proverb

In the northwest corner of our basement in Indiana, I have set up a small medical museum. Mary believes that such weird and dangerous old tools of the medical profession are not appropriate to display where visitors might stumble onto them. So I take those who express an interest to the very back of the basement, behind a portable room divider decorated by Mary with artificial vines. I have never bought any of this antique equipment or any of the obsolete medicines and doctor bags, but over the years friends and patients have given them to me as curiosities that have been passed down in their families from some past physician. The local hospital in Bluffton, Indiana, presented some of the museum pieces to me when they cleaned out corners of their building.

Each shelf of the old medicine cabinet, which itself dates back eighty years, contains an assortment of instruments relating to one specific area of medicine. The top shelf holds instruments related to obstetrical care. Pelvic speculums reveal radical changes in design over the past century, and pelvic forceps lay next to an antiquated rectal ether machine. The next shelf down exhibits instruments for performing tonsillectomies and adenoidectomies. Other shelves reveal the development of scissors, hemostats, orthopedic instruments, and so on. These items may only be seventy-five to a hundred years old, but they stimulate my curiosity and increase my admiration for those physicians who paved the way before me.

When I graduated from medical school in 1963, I thought medicine had nearly reached its pinnacle, that it had advanced to the point where few future changes would be required. We had developed medicines for most illnesses, antibiotics to treat infections, and I had just participated in one of the first reported successful closed heart resuscitations. Doctor Salk had recently developed the polio vaccine that was wiping out that dreaded disease. Those were hopeful times.

Now I look back over the past forty years and realize that what I learned in medical school was just the beginning of modern medicine. The rate of progress in medicine and medical technology just keeps accelerating and the advances expanding. Twenty years into the future . . . what changes will occur? I think, then, of how insignificant my role in medicine has really been. Future physicians will reflect on these decades as a rather primitive era. There is only one important discovery in my medical experience I can point to and say I found something new, something previously unknown in medical history. This discovery occurred during my year in Somalia.

Our area of southern Somalia, by the Juba River, was one of the pockets with the highest incidence of malaria in the world. Every missionary took malaria prophylaxis, one pill weekly. We witnessed patients with all three types of the malaria organisms in our area. Plasmodium vivax was the most common, but we also encountered Plasmodium falciform and Plasmodium malaria. The malaria patients we saw were often acutely ill with high fever, severe aching, chilling, and vomiting. Infected children were frequently brought in dehydrated and in a coma.

Some extremely ill patients developed central nervous system problems, with hallucinations and severe headaches, along with other conventional symptoms of malaria. When patients exhibited chronic malaria or suffered recurrent attacks, they developed enlarged spleens and became anemic. They ran a chronic low grade fever and experienced weakness and fatigue. I could merely look at them and make the diagnosis. They appeared pale, with a large, protruding abdomen and scars from where the bush doctors had burned them. We treated these patients with chloroquin, either with tablets or intravenously, and many of the severely ill made a quick recovery.

During the rainy season, when the incidence of malaria was highest, I noticed that many babies died in the hospital twenty-four to forty-eight hours after a normal delivery. I also heard in the community that this was occurring with home deliveries as well. The medical literature at that time indicated that the plasmodium organism did not cross the placental barrier from mother to child while the fetus was in the uterus. I searched for the reason these babies, healthy at delivery, were dying so soon after birth and discussed this with the malaria division of UNICEF in Somalia. But the organization offered no real help.

I decided that with every hospital birth we would check the umbilical cord blood at delivery. We made two slides, one we examined in our lab and one we collected for UNICEF. Because we were located in an endemic area for malaria, it did not take us long to discover that the plasmodium organism was, indeed, crossing the placental barrier. We even sometimes found the malaria organism in the cord blood when both the mother's and baby's smears were negative. Sometimes all three would be positive.

Knowing this, we started chloroquin treatment on any woman who arrived for delivery and soon discovered that these tragic neonatal deaths decreased dramatically. UNICEF agreed with our finding, and I witnessed a correction in the following medical literature, indicating that malaria can pass through the placental barrier. That was my discovery for the advancement of medicine.

CHAPTER THIRTY

One should neither be late for the wedding nor stay too long at it.
—Somali Proverb

When Mary and I were married in 1956, we followed the Mennonite tradition of not exchanging rings, and Mary carried a small white Bible with a few red roses rather than a bouquet. But, like the general American populace, we decided to have bridesmaids and groomsmen, and Mary wore a wedding gown, though not a veil. One change was simply our own: We decided to face the congregation since it didn't seem right to turn our backs to family and friends. Another change Mary made was to omit the word *obey* when she spoke her traditional marriage vow. But this was unconscious. Neither she nor I even realized the omission until after the service when the minister brought it up. For more than fifty years, however, Mary has maintained that her memory lapse improved the wording.

When we were in Somalia, a land steeped in tradition, young engaged couples didn't have as much choice as we did in planning their wedding. Not much changes from one generation to the next in the ceremonies that Somalis hold dearest.

I learned that it was imperative that the young woman to be married be a virgin. By puberty or as young as five or six years of age, she would have received a clitorectomy, with the lower portion of the vulva sewed shut to leave only a small opening for urine or menstrual flow. Several weeks before the wedding, the future mother-in-law would cut open the vulva of the girl to assure that the groom was, indeed, marrying a virgin. Sometimes, though, the young women were brought to the clinic for my examination. Pale and sweaty, these girls waited in fear of what I might determine. If I said a girl was still a virgin, then she could get married. If I said she was not, then she would be labeled a prostitute for the rest of her life. She would never be able to marry, her family would disown her, and she would end up poor and miserable.

As mentioned earlier, because I was an infidel, I could perform a pelvic on these young women, but no male Muslim doctor or nurse could administer the examination. If I had not been there, some older woman in the community would have determined the outcome for these young women. Frequently, the previous clitorectomies were so poorly performed that it was impossible to tell for sure if the woman was, indeed, a virgin so during my tenure I found all the young women to be virgins.

When Lul, our receptionist at the hospital, was getting married, all of the mission personnel were invited. Since the marriage of young people is parentally arranged in Somalia, I don't really know whether Lul knew her fiancé before the wedding, although I would see a few of the young nursing students and their boyfriends holding hands at some events.

I was invited to Lul's wedding and marriage feast and to another wedding of a young Arab couple from the village but was unable to attend either event. Mary, however, attended both weddings, or rather, wedding feasts, because only the groom and male family and friends are part of the formal marriage ceremony. A male relative of the bride, usually her father, acts as her representative. Not having grown up in the Somali culture, Mary could not understand the significance of all the activities at the wedding feasts, but she felt honored to have been invited and has written down what she remembers of the events.

As we entered the courtyard at Lul's parents' home, the other missionary women and I walked under an arch of palm branches which looked refreshing with everything else brown and dry. Then we were ushered into one of the houses and seated at a table with chairs. As Westerners, we were given big tablespoons to eat with, but the Somali women sat on floor mats and ate the traditional way, with their fingers. We were served delicious goat meat with rice and, to drink, Sprite or orange Fanta. After we finished eating, we were passed a bowl of water to rinse our hands and a towel to dry them. As a last act of hospitality, fragrant cologne was poured over our hands.

Across the courtyard, in another house, the women were congregating in a circle, chanting a prayer to Allah to make this marriage a happy one. Earlier, during the meal, I had asked where Lul was and had learned that she was at a friend's house because a bride must not be seen in public during her wedding festivities, a series of activities that last three days.

In the late afternoon, about five o'clock, all the women on the mission staff walked to Lul's friend's house to see the bride and to give her gifts. Upon entering her room, we took off our shoes and sat on a floor mat. The only other furnishings in the room were a bed on which the bride was seated and a record player. First, we were served strong Somali coffee and then a large, red mound of helwa, from which each of us pulled off a piece to eat. Helwa is a sticky, sweet candy that resembles thick jelly.

Following the coffee and helwa, we went into the courtyard, where the women danced in a circle, clapping their hands with a drummer while the family's goats watched in the background. After a while, the women put on some James Brown records and started doing American dances. Soon they wanted me to show them some new steps, but since I don't know any dances, I refrained.

Several weeks later, Martha, Pauline, and I journeyed into the village to one of the Arab homes for a wedding feast. It seems strange to go to these celebrations and not see any men. When we arrived, many of the women were assembled in the courtyard, dancing to the drums, but we were escorted inside to one of the rooms and given chairs. They passed us a small dish of water to wash the one hand with which we would be eating. I went first and washed both of mine because I didn't know any better. This made the water a little extra cloudy for the two other women.

We were then served rice, goat meat, helwa, coffee, biscuits, and soft drinks. This was the first time I was served rice and meat without any utensils. I watched the nurses as they took a handful of rice, squeezed it together into a ball, and rolled it down to the end of their four fingers cupped to make a scoop. We ate a lot because one of the Arab women sitting with us kept insisting that we eat more and more. After we finished with spicy coffee, they closed the outside door to the curious, onlooking women and children, and brought out a big, beautiful box of assorted chocolates from Italy.

Following our meal, we took our chairs to the courtyard to watch the dancing. Two women at a time got up, took off their black shukas (the black wrap that covers Arab women from top to bottom when they go out in public), put a band of bells around their ankles, and began dancing. It was interesting to see all the jewelry that the dancers were wearing—lots of genuine gold. These Arab women had much more money than the average Jamama woman because their husbands were the merchants of the village. One woman did a fascinating dance in which she let down her long black hair and then put her head back, turning it from side to side, faster and faster, until the hair was flying.

Before we left, our hostesses invited us into the bride's room, where the bride is kept out of sight. This happened to be a double wedding. There were two beds or cots, a bride on each one, and each bride was completely covered by a blanket. The brides uncovered their heads just long enough to shake hands with us. They looked sad, and I was told that brides were supposed to show sorrow on their wedding day.

As we walked home, one of the nurses told me that the reason brides are so sad is because, when girls reach puberty, the old aunts or grandmothers sew their vaginas shut with elephant hair and, when they are ready for marriage, someone from the groom's family takes a razor blade to open the vagina. This also tells the groom that his fiancée is a virgin. By this time, the skin has grown together, making the procedure a painful one.

CHAPTER THIRTY-ONE

In good times be ready for bad times.
—Somali Proverb

Mary and I made arrangements to travel to Nairobi before Easter to spend one week with our daughters and my parents before Rosslyn Academy closed for Spring Break. The girls would then return with us to Somalia.

However, on March 5, one week before we were to leave, I received a telegram from the District Court in Kismayu informing me that I was to appear eight days later in court. It did not tell me what the court case was in reference to. I had been to court several times to give testimony concerning the injuries of patients who had come to the hospital, to provide verification that a girl was still a virgin, and one time to help in a matter of conflict between two wives of the same man. So I thought this was nothing out of the ordinary.

Hassen Nur, my hospital administrator and interpreter, went with me to ask the judge to change the date of my court appearance so that I could still keep my travel plans.

The judge told me, "I cannot change the date because you are being charged with the murder of Hussein Sadad Hassen." He added, "If you leave the country, you will be running from prosecution and will, therefore, be considered guilty."

What a shock. We had gone to see the judge for what I thought would be a routine request for me to give testimony. Now I was the one accused . . . and of murder. Hassen Nur said very little but indicated that he was also surprised and did not really know what this meant. He had never heard of a physician being accused of murder for taking care of a sick patient. Before we started back, Hassen and I prayed together, asking God for understanding and guidance in this matter. It was a long, quiet ride back to Jamama that afternoon. I just couldn't understand how something like this could happen. My relationship with the government and community leaders had always seemed amiable during the past eight months. I felt bewildered and disoriented—how a nomad must feel who travels to a familiar watering hole, only to discover it filled with dust.

When we arrived back at the mission compound, the other personnel started giving me support and encouragement. I heard for the first time that Dr. Kratz, the previous physician, had also gone to court when someone had accused him of injury. His crime was that he disposed of a placenta after a delivery instead of giving it to the family for a religious ceremony in which it is buried. After going to trial, he was found innocent. But *murder*—that seemed a more serious matter, like a sandstorm that could engulf you.

The United States government did not recognize the government of Somalia, and, therefore, had no embassy in the country. We contacted our mission administrator in Mogadishu, Harold Reed, and he put me in touch with a lawyer whom the mission had previously used. Several days later, I went to Mogadishu to meet with this man.

The lawyer's office was on the second floor of a building in the city's downtown. The waiting room was small with a few empty chairs, and the receptionist was a pleasant young woman who greeted me in English. After a fifteen-minute wait, I met the gentleman who would be my lawyer. He was a man in his mid-fifties who spoke fairly fluent British English. I felt reassured that he understood the circumstances of Hussein's accident and death.

Hassen Scek Ibrahim agreed to take my case and to find out the accusations concerning the murder charges. He told me he would change the date of the trial and that I should go on to Nairobi for the week to see my daughters and parents. He would contact me when I returned. So, at the last minute, I did travel to Kenya with Mary and Stephen.

This was a time when praying came easily and frequently, which was good because, after that first meeting with the judge, I felt less sure of myself and more in need of help. Fortunately, my wife and the Mennonite community in Somalia were extremely supportive during this time. They gave encouragement and were never critical of anything I had done. Only later would our family and friends in Indiana hear of these charges, but, for the present, I relied on the support of missionaries throughout East Africa.

In the past, I felt called to pray at meetings for other mission workers and the Somali people, but I would only pray for myself in private. Now I was the recipient of prayer, and my family was listed specifically on prayer lists. I could feel that support, like a gourd filled with cool water, and it gave me great peace. Still, though, it was hard to turn the situation over to God and not worry.

When I returned from Kenya, I again met with my attorney and he told me the trial would take place on March 23. He didn't have much to say about the charges, only that there was nothing we needed to prepare for and that I shouldn't worry. So I waited and prayed. During this time, the Somali missions held their yearly spiritual retreat at Jowhar where a large secondary school was located. The theme of the three-day conference was "Our God is Able." The timing was perfect, and my spirits were lifted as we sang hymns and choruses, prayed, and listened to Hershey Leaman, from Nairobi, speak on "Creative Christianity in a Muslim culture."

We ended the conference by singing, "On Christ the solid rock I stand," and that is where I put my trust. However, being in a foreign culture and not knowing what might happen in the trial, I worried about the next phrase in the song: "all other ground is sinking sand." Whenever we trudged over sand dunes to reach the beach, our feet sinking out of sight, Chester, with his deep baritone, would sing that chorus. I had an inward peace, but sometimes I would experience a sinking feeling and anxiety about the trial. I had no idea of what to expect.

I'm with my prized Guernsey, Betty, before taking her to show at the State Fair in Indianapolis. At this point in my life, I wanted to be a veterinarian.

This stately camel grazes on a bush outside of Jamama. Camels, which are bred for milk and carrying burdens, are a Somali's most valued possession.

At our first destination—Nairobi, Kenya. My parents, Perry J. and Lucile, taught at Rosslyn Academy, the same school where Shari and Marlis boarded.

A sign for the Somalia Mennonite Mission in Somalia's capital, the ancient coastal city of Mogadishu.

Above: *A white minaret rises from the midst of Kismayu's tin and thatched roofs.*
Below: *When in public, the Arab women in Jamama always wore a covering called a shuka. This mother and child are on their way to the clinic.*

A quiet residential street in Jamama. Branch enclosures protect young trees from roaming livestock.

Somali children spend most of their free time out-doors and with friends.

Lorries are the most common form of mass transit from one Somali village to another.

A view of Jamama's business district.

My first cataract patient (right) after a successful surgery.

Pauline Zimmerman and the public health outreach team before going out to give immunizations. Asli Aden Ashkir, a nursing student now living in the U.S., is third from left. Behind her stands Hussein, a nurse practitioner and screener.

Women dressed in traditional wrap-arounds. Lul, the receptionist at the hospital, is standing at center; Mariam Mohamed Hassen, a nursing student, is on the right.

Second from right is my good friend Hassen Nur, the hospital administrator. Abdi Gure, who assisted with surgeries and ran the pharmacy, is second from left.

Our family visits the home of Mohamed Aden, a nurse who assisted me with cataract surgeries.

Hawa helped Mary with housekeeping and baking. Here she is with her husband and young son.

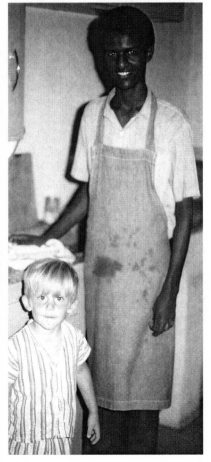

Above: *Stephen holds Abdi Hakim, his baby brother for a year.*

Left: *After his school day is over, Omar works in our home. Eventually, Omar became a nurse and was asked to lead a new nursing program at Somali University.*

Akim Siad on a visit with family members to see his son, Abdi.

Above: *Elsie Van Pelt borrows Abdi to demonstrate to students on how to safely bathe an infant.* Below: *Mary, Stephen and Abdi spend an afternoon visiting Hawa at her home.*

Above left: *Shari with her favorite pet on the compound—Jack, a Vervet monkey.*
Above right: *I'm giving a bottle of milk to Stephen's baby baboon.*

*Stephen's climbing tree, an acacia, in the foreground,
and his playhouse in the background.*

Right: *Marlis with a pet goat and rabbit.* Below: *This elderly camel is brought to our door with the hope that Mary might buy him.*

Two camels walking through downtown Jamama.

Above: *Mary with (from left to right) Catherine Kurtz, Elsie Cressman, Martha Horst, and Pauline Zimmerman before they depart for a wedding feast.*

Community people gather to watch dancers during a celebration of the Revolution's second anniversary.

Right:
Mission personnel pose on the monument that marks the equator. We drove past this marker every time we took a trip from Jamama to Kismayu.

Below:
A coral reef at low tide. We collected shells here and watched bright tropical fish in the scattered pools.

After a picnic of spicy zamboozies, Mary and Stephen relax on the Kismayu beach.

Above: *The Juba River during the rainy season. This river was Jamama's lifeline, supplying water for irrigation, drinking, and bathing.*
Below: *Here our family is all together . . . thirty-five years later.*

PART THREE

"Allah himself helps a simple man to find a good place for his camp."

—*Somali Proverb*

CHAPTER THIRTY-TWO

A word is like a sinew: it stretches in every direction.
—Somali Proverb

The District Court of Kismayu served the southern district of Somalia and was housed in a one-story building of light red mud plastered over exterior cement blocks. It stood at the edge of the city on a slight rise overlooking the Indian Ocean. Two acacia trees canopied the front, and, as with other buildings and homes, there was no yard. The dirt path to the entrance was well swept and marked by white-washed rocks along each side. Ibraham, my lawyer, was waiting at the double door when Hassen Nur and I arrived, and he told me how he expected the trial would be handled by the judge.

"All three defendants will be tried together—you, Dr. Urquhart and the driver of the car—," he explained, "but you will each be asked different questions. There will be a court interpreter who will translate everything into English so you will be able to understand the proceedings. The judge has scheduled this for a one-day trial."

From the front doors, we entered directly into the courtroom, a large room, bare-walled except for the grim photograph of General Mohamed Siad Barre mounted on the front wall above the judge's table. The two windows on each side of the room were open. By eight a.m., when the board benches filled and people crowded around the edges of the room, I could see curious individuals standing three deep, peering in from outside. For the next couple of hours, the other two defendants and I, who were seated on a bench to the right of the judge's table, waited for the judge to arrive while the board grew harder and my anxiety more intense.

At ten-thirty we all stood when the judge in his black robe strode into the room. He sat at the table, looking very stern as he thumbed through a stack of papers. Dr. Urquhart and I were being accused of the murder of Hussein Sadad Hassen, and the driver of the car, Mohamed Abdi Warsame, was also being accused of his murder and of causing the injuries of the two female passengers.

Dr. Urquhart and the driver had hired the same attorney though, during the trial, I never heard their lawyer speak. Ibraham, my lawyer, sat beside me, but he was not asked any questions and was also given little opportunity to talk. He did frequently translate into clearer English what the judge and district prosecuting attorney were asking me.

The court proceedings, which seemed to progress slowly, did last only one day. Much of the time was spent translating questions and answers from one language to another. Five languages were used that day in the courtroom. The southern half of Somalia, where we were located, had previously been Italian Somaliland, and that included the capital, Mogadishu. So there was considerable Italian spoken in the region, and the legal system, which deemed I was guilty until proven innocent, was founded on Italian jurisprudence.Frequently, the judge appeared to be looking up references in thick legal books I assumed were Italian. Somali was also used in the courtroom, but, at that time, it was still an unwritten language. Everything was translated into Arabic because the typewriter was Arabic, so that was the language of record keeping. All of the records from the hospital were in English, and an interpreter translated every spoken Somali word into English for my benefit. The autopsy report and the Russian doctor's review of our hospital records were in Russian.

So, Italian, Somali, Arabic, English and Russian all played a role in the same courtroom. It was easy to lose something in the translation and hard to follow through with a single thought or question. We spent a lot of time agreeing on the exact time the surgery started and stopped and at what exact moment Dr. Urqhuart arrived at the hospital and left.

We also spent time discussing the injuries to the two women in the car, their condition and diagnosis when they arrived at the hospital, and the duration of their stay. But mostly the prosecuting attorney wanted to know about Hussein's injuries. What were they and how did we treat them? He called Pauline, the American nurse present during the surgery, to read most of the record for the last twenty-four hours of the patient's life, and every word had to be translated into Somali and Arabic. Several of the Somali nurses also testified as to their presence during Hussein's surgery. The prosecuting attorney was particularly concerned about the exact time everything was done. He was also concerned about where everyone stood during the surgery, and, since three months had passed, the nurses had a hard time giving exact locations.

The prosecuting attorney then presented the Russian doctor's findings, but he was only concerned with the final cause of death that appeared in his report. The patient died of "shock." This diagnosis concurred with our hospital records; however, our records also recorded why Hussein died of shock.

I was not sure how the judge and prosecuting attorney interpreted *shock*, as they both kept repeating the word. I tried to explain what had happened to Hussein during and after the surgery that contributed to the clinical definition of shock. All of their questions that day were directed toward me and not the other two defendants, and our understanding of certain words or phrases in the English language could have different meanings or connotations in Somali or Arabic. For instance, early in the trial, the judge asked me, "How long have you been a doctor?"

I replied, "I have been practicing medicine for ten years."

He exclaimed, "Oh, so you are here practicing on us. You are not a real doctor."

I tried to explain the use of the word *practice* in the United States, that as doctors of medicine, everything we do as physicians is considered "practicing." I told him he would be practicing law as I was practicing medicine. The judge was rather indignant and replied, "I *perform* law and do not practice. I know the difference between practicing and performing." And that's the way the whole day went.

The court case was over at five p.m., and the judge's last words to me were, "You will return in ten days, and I will have the judgment and sentencing." As we were leaving, Ibraham indicated that everything had gone well and he expected I would be acquitted. He saw no reason why he should make the flight from Mogadishu for the judgment and then wait three days to make the return flight when there was no question as to the outcome.

I returned to Jamama that evening feeling somewhat relieved, but still anxious because, in a foreign culture, things are not always as they appear.

CHAPTER THIRTY-THREE

The world is like a shadow: in the morning it is turned toward one direction, in the evening toward the opposite one.
—Somali Proverb

When you are waiting for a murder verdict, ten days inch by like a tree's shadow with the movement of the sun. As the time drew near, I had the sense, though, that my lawyer was right: everything would work out; justice would prevail.

On the day of the sentencing, Hassen Nur and I arrived at the courthouse at eight in the morning. Dr. Urquhart, the driver, and I again sat on the same bench in the same room, but this time there were only a couple dozen onlookers. We were asked to stand as the judge entered the room, and we sat down as he, again, spent considerable time thumbing through paperwork.

He commanded each of us to stand as he read through the verdict and sentencing, starting with the driver: "The accident took place because the driver was imprudent and negligent and was driving the vehicle at a harsh speed at a turning point. Therefore, he is given a suspended six month sentence and is ordered to pay damages to Fatuma Abdulle and Lul Abduraham. He will need to pay their hospital bills and give them some compensation for their injuries. However, he is not responsible for the death of Hassan Sadad Hussein because the victim was in a stable condition before the surgery.

"Dr. Urquhart performed the surgery, but because he performed it correctly and the patient was out of danger when Dr. Urquhart left the hospital, he cannot be held guilty.

"Dr. Miller was in charge of the hospital and of the patient's care. The records show that the patient died of 'shock,' and, even though we cannot find anything that Dr. Miller did wrong, he had the duty of taking care of him after the surgery. Also, for a long time the patient was in Dr. Miller's care, so he should have known of his condition and was negligent in allowing the surgery.

"Therefore, we find Dr. Miller guilty of the death of Hussein Sadad Hassan and sentence him to three months in prison. He is also to compensate the family of the deceased by giving the family one hundred camels. But, because he is needed at the Jamama Hospital, he will not have to serve the prison term as long as he stays in the country and does nothing wrong for the next five years. However, if he has a subsequent charge brought against him, then he will have to serve the prison term."

The judge pronounced this in Arabic and did not have it translated into English. Following the verdict, he rose and left the room. The driver and his friend rose and left the room also. Dr. Urquhart and I discussed the unexpected sentencing as best we understood it. He told me to appeal the verdict because it wasn't just. We shook hands, and I never saw him again. Soon afterward, he closed his hospital and clinic in Kismayu and departed to Mombasa, Kenya, on a permanent basis.

Hassen Nur made copies of the verdict and sentencing, and we sent a copy to Harold and one to our lawyer in Mogadishu. We then drove back to Jamama, past the dry *guban* with its desolate miles of sand in every direction and its villages, now distant and deserted, in the glare of late morning sun. Baobabs, like upside down trees with roots stuck in the air, were part of a bad dream I wanted to wake up from.

As soon as I could, I had the verdict and sentencing translated into English so we could understand the full meaning. I wondered, however, about the accuracy of the translation when I read that I was born in Gosher, India. I also noticed in this document that the judge had written, "the car that overturned was going a harsh speed of Kms. 100 per hr. The accident took place at a turning point at which there were not traffic signals." No mention was made of the fact that the driver had consumed alcohol before driving, only that "some bottles containing beverages were found in the car" and that the two women, as injured parties, "did not say that the driver was drunk."

I also noticed in the records that, although I was accused of criminal homicide, there was never any mention of possible motive and that the only evidence of my guilt was that the patient had died of shock. The papers indicated that "the patient was out of danger" after the surgery. But that, of course, was not true. The verdict explained that although my actions did "not seem a criminal act according to the evidence given by witnesses, the documents and the particular autopsy and the register of the hospital and the clinical card of the patient seem to be contradicting with the witnesses." According to the judge, "The medical evidence shows that the cause of death was a shock due to the surgical operation, but did not mention the grounds and whether an indispensable technical rule was neglected. . . . Anyway one thing is certain and that is that before the operation there was no danger of death for the defunct, and, therefore, death might be caused by surgical intervention, so the penal responsibility may still exist. . . ." Although I was found guilty of criminal homicide, my crime "was not to be mentioned in the criminal record office."

Over the next couple of weeks, I communicated with Harold, he communicated with his superiors at the mission headquarters in Kenya, and they in turn conversed with the leadership and board in Pennsylvania. The decision delivered to me was that I should meet with Hussein's family and the mission would pay the blood money—the value of one hundred camels. The Board of Missions would then have me switch places with a doctor from the mission hospital in Uganda for the remainder of my term.

The option of appealing the verdict to a higher court was a possibility that had been discussed. My trial had been in a district court; the next court would be the regional and then, if necessary, the final appeal would be to the National Supreme Court. Although this option was discussed at all levels of the mission board in Somalia, Kenya, and Pennsylvania, it was rejected because Mennonites have traditionally tried to avoid litigation. We feel it is important to live by the teaching of Jesus as recorded in the Sermon on the Mount in Matthew, chapter five: "But I say to you, do not resist one who is evil. But if anyone strikes you on the right cheek, turn to him the other also; and if anyone would sue you and take your coat, let him have your cloak as well." Mennonites realize that the world needs laws and courts, but, in our personal lives, we try to live peaceably with all people. If we are accused falsely, we are to accept the accusation with humility and, if possible, to attempt reconciliation.

Of course, it concerned me that a court of law had found me guilty of criminal homicide. And as family and friends in Indiana started hearing of the sentencing judgment, I started receiving letters suggesting I come back immediately to the States. "You have been trying to help them and now see what they have done to you," wrote one person. However, most people understood the circumstances and just offered moral support and prayers. My wife and the Mennonite community in Somalia were very supportive during this time. I did not feel like a murderer, and, of course, I did not think of myself as one. I tried to maintain perspective, remembering the words of my attorney: "This is a very light sentence."

Still, I couldn't help wondering how enforceable the provision of the sentence was that stipulated I could not leave the country for five years. Would I even be allowed to go to Uganda to trade places with another doctor? All I knew for sure was that my part of the sentencing involved meeting with the family of Hussein to settle the blood money.

I had seen the outside of the prisons in Mogadishu and Kismayu with their ten foot high walls topped with rows of curly barbed-wire. I had heard that most people inside die of tuberculosis or other illnesses. Medical treatment is not available, everyone lives in close proximity, and food is scarce.

CHAPTER THIRTY-FOUR

News hurries to a meeting place.
—Somali Proverb

After the sentencing, I sensed a different atmosphere in Jamama and in the surrounding villages. Villagers who had seemed reserved were now more pleasant and many of the community leaders stopped by the hospital to express concern and to offer their help. Before the trial, the hospital had always been the American Mission Hospital, but now people in Jamama referred to it as *their* hospital. The clinic was busier than any time during the past year. One morning we had 180 visits and forty-five later in the day. Everyone seemed to know about the court case, even the nomads who came through in their camel caravans. There were no newspapers, but the story spread quickly by word of mouth.

At one point during the weeks after the sentencing, Hassen Nur and I found ourselves at a secret midnight meeting. It occurred rather innocently. Hassen Nur approached me one day and said, "This morning several leaders in Jamama came to my office and asked if we would come to a meeting. They want to discuss how this verdict is going to affect the hospital and would like you and me to attend if at all possible. I don't suppose it would hurt. What do you think?" I indicated that it might be wise to see what the community leaders were thinking. But I was surprised they were holding the meeting so late at night. It didn't start until eleven.

Hassen Nur arrived at our house at 10:30, and he and I started off to the meeting place in the village. The night was dark, with only a sliver of moon showing. A few stragglers stirred in the courtyards, but otherwise the streets were quiet. The town's generator, which supplied electricity for a few low-powered street lights and special buildings, had already been switched off. Hassen led me through several different streets and then down paths that in the dark I did not recognize.

Finally we arrived at a courtyard outside a large house. We were greeted at the gate, led into the house, and shown into a spacious room illuminated only by the small floor lanterns that burned in each corner. It was hard to distinguish anyone with the flickering shadows that leapt across faces and walls. Hassen Nur seemed to know a few of the men present, but I did not recognize anyone. We were offered chairs in the back of the room, but most of the men were seated on the floor. The meeting had obviously started before we arrived. I knew nothing about what they were discussing, but after about ten minutes Hassen whispered in my ear, "We should not be here. Let us leave now, and I will explain to you outside." He said something to a few of the men beside us, obviously excusing us, and we got up, hurriedly leaving the room and the house.

After we had exited the courtyard, Hassen explained why we had left so abruptly. "We should not have gone to the meeting," he said. "This is an underground organization that is trying to overthrow the government. They wanted to use your trial to strengthen their efforts. It is good we left when we did." We walked home in silence, both of us, I imagine, contemplating what would have happened had we gotten involved with such a radical organization.

Word of the verdict and sentencing had now reached our family, church, and medical practice in the States. Because our friends and family were so far away and not involved in the case, they had considerable anxiety. Dr. Kinzer from our medical practice called the U.S. State Department and tried to contact Ambassador E. Ross Adair in Ethiopia. The State Department was concerned, but they were not sure how they could help since the U.S. did not recognize the Somali government.

CHAPTER THIRTY-FIVE

What is nourishing in appearance is nourishing indeed.
—Somali Proverb

Even though a court of law had found me guilty of causing Hussein's death, I felt assured that I had done everything I could do for him while he was alive. At least everything I could do in Somalia. After the initial shock of the verdict, I gradually gained a sense of inward peace, though sometimes it was gnawed by uncertainty, by what the verdict might mean for the future of the hospital and the mission and for my situation in the country.

During this time, I appreciated the prayers and concern of other mission workers, but I was also grateful that they did not continually bring up the trial and verdict like a useless bucket of sand from a well but let life on the compound go on as usual. It was helpful to be kept busy with all the medical work and teaching. However, sometimes I needed to just get away by myself to meditate or plan for the future. In the States, I found my morning and evening commute to and from the hospital and office to be such a time. I would reflect on the condition of patients or upcoming problems. I would take that time to pray or to even memorize portions of the Bible. Mary said she worried about my driving skills when I had so much on my mind.

In Somalia, I did not have those long drives. The best time for reflection was at night when the generator had been turned off and I could sit outside beneath the star-lit sky, contemplating God's amazing creation. The Somalis have a folktale that stars were created by two women pounding millet with a mortar and pestle. They weren't careful, and the shaft of their pestle poked holes in the sky. In fact, the Somali word for sky is *daldaloole*, "the holed thing." I had never viewed so many holes in the sky, and they had never appeared so close. I could imagine Abraham or Jacob lying in a desert land, beneath such a bright tent of a sky, and I knew the awe that they must have felt.

At times during the year I could see some of the familiar constellations of the Northern Hemisphere, but usually I saw ones of the Southern Hemisphere. I didn't know most of their names, but I could always find the Southern Cross. Sometimes a meteorite shower would startle the universe for a moment. Beneath the night sky, my thoughts would gain the proper perspective, and I would know what to do next.

Another place I found solace was at the beach. As a family or as a group from the compound, we would venture to the Indian Ocean for an afternoon. The white shoreline was usually empty, and there was no pressure to communicate or help someone else. I could just relax and enjoy the sand and the drone of the sea. Early in the afternoon, when the sand became too hot to walk on barefoot, we could stroll along the edge of the foamy water or go for a swim.

On our way to or from the beach, there were often moments, however, that weren't relaxing. The Fiat would get stuck in drifts of sand, and then some of us would pile out to push. One time, I leaped out barefooted to push and, as the vehicle picked up speed to escape other drifts, I was left stranded in the hot sand. I tried to run fast over the surface but had to sporadically stop to dig my feet deeper into cooler sand. That night I had blisters from second-degree burns on the bottom of my feet. That was the last time I got out to push without my shoes.

But the water of the Indian Ocean was mesmerizing—a deep blue with low waves melting into ripples for as far as I could see. Large ships or fishing boats often skimmed along the horizon. Once, we saw a small Persian dhow come sailing from the distance right up to our shore. A man jumped out, carrying a live lobster over three feet long. The fisherman did not speak English, but I bought his catch for fourteen shillings or two dollars. At home, the lobster was so large Mary and I couldn't submerge all of it in our wash tub at one time.

There was always a refreshing breeze at the ocean. In the clear water, we'd search for cowries, their shiny shells spotted like the coats of Dalmatians or laced with delicate patterns. The ocean floor was fairly flat, and when the tide was out, we could walk for a fourth of a mile on the coral, looking for shells. But we also had to be wary of sea urchins; we didn't want their sharp spines lodged in our feet or ankles.

Playing the card game Rook around the kerosene lantern at night was also a diversion that took my mind off the trial and later the verdict. Martha would often come over to our house when the lights went off, and for one to two hours we all played Rook. Sometimes Pauline or Elsie would join us, and, when Shari and Marlis were home, they also played. Thursday and Saturday nights were especially good nights for a card game because we could sleep in later the next morning.

Mary and I grew up playing Rook as children and then played with our extended family at gatherings. Traditionally, it has been a favorite among Mennonites since it lacks the face cards associated with gambling. At a young age, our oldest daughter, Shari, learned her numbers from one to fourteen while watching Mary and me play with our Mennonite friends in medical school. It was in Somalia where we learned to play "The Bird" low, at ten and a half points, and to use a double deck if we were playing with more than five people.

Chess matches with Chester also challenged and diverted my mind. Chess was a new game for me when we arrived, but one that most of the missionaries, especially the men, played. Interestingly enough, it was a game that was in the international news throughout 1972, as the twenty-nine-year-old Chicago-born prodigy, Bobby Fischer, took on Boris Spassky in an attempt to reverse the Soviet domination of chess. With chess, I could still carry on a conversation or plan the next day's activities. I could stop for a hospital emergency and return later to finish the game. At first Chester would always win, but I soon learned to avoid the moves that had previously placed my King in jeopardy.

Chess could distract thoughts about the verdict, but many times I needed exercise to relax the tension in my body, and tennis was that sport. When we first arrived, Chester had already cleared an area in front of his house of grass and had set up posts and a net. I helped him paint the lines, but every time we played, we first had to sweep off the loose sand to see those lines and to reach the firm, smooth surface underneath. It didn't take us long to learn that it was best to start playing after four p.m., when the day was beginning to cool.

Eating out can be a way to relax, but there were no steakhouses or fast food restaurants in Jamama, and the little downtown café was not a safe place to eat. Our best option for eating out was to take our own picnic to a banana plantation or *ascenda*. We usually went as a mission family to celebrate a birthday, an anniversary, or a holiday. I have discovered in my travels that in many places, the poorer the nation, the greater the need for holidays. The plantations we would visit were usually owned and farmed by second- or third-generation Italians who had grown up in Somalia. The Italians at these ascendas were Catholic but very supportive of our mission. I would see them in the clinics for non-life-threatening illnesses or emergencies. For surgeries or for severe illnesses, they returned to Italy where their children attended secondary school.

These ascendas were located along the Juba River so that farmers could engineer canals to irrigate the banana fields. We could spread out our blankets and unpack our baskets beneath a grove of palm trees or a large, spreading baobab. We might enjoy the brilliant orange flowers of the flamboyant tree or the fragrance of white frangipani blossoms. We might marvel at the bottle brush tree, at its strange red bristles. Many trees imported from other tropical countries thrived in these irrigated oases. Often we saw flowering hibiscus and bougainvillea bushes and sometimes a pond with catfish. These picnics provided a welcome retreat from the stress of the hospital, clinic, and school . . . and now the court's verdict.

CHAPTER THIRTY-SIX

When you see that everything becomes dry, expect rain.
—Somali Proverb

It was late March . . . and still no rain. Everyone was talking about the fact that it had been ten months since the last precipitation. That really wasn't accurate since we had ten minutes of moisture in November during what was supposed to have been the autumn rainy season. Rain was on everyone's mind as Somalis spoke of years when they did not have even spring rains. Now the ground was hard and cracked; sand swirled and drifted. All Somalia was dry. Finally, we heard rumors from passing nomads that neighboring Ethiopia had received some rainfall and that it might be headed toward us.

When we started to see the Juba River rising, everyone started looking for rain clouds. Several weeks passed, though, before we saw them over Jamama. Farmers hoed their gardens and small fields so they would be ready to plant when the rains came. Mary's father, a farmer, always looked upward in late June and July, wondering if his corn would dry up or if rain clouds would bring a bumper crop. But in Somalia the lack of water was more dire. The cattle were starving from a dearth of grass, and grain had long since disappeared.

Before the drought, I had routinely seen children in the clinic with kwashiorkor disease, a protein deficiency. These children exhibited swelling of the arms, legs, and face with a large, protuberant abdomen. Their hair often turned red and their skin would crack over their joints. These symptoms probably suggested more than a mere protein deficiency, however, since the children also lacked vitamins and minerals. They were getting enough calories but not enough variety in their diet.

Now we were also seeing children with marasmus, a progressive wasting and emaciation. The word, in fact, means "dying away." The condition especially affected two to ten-year-olds. After these toddlers stopped breast-feeding, with no other food source available, they gradually starved to death. This was first seen among the very poor, but now, since there hadn't been any rains and there was little to buy in the way of food, even if you had something to sell or barter, starvation was afflicting more young children of all social classes. Unless they are suffering from a disease that depletes their bodies, older children and adults will last longer with less food. But if children up to four years of age develop kwashiorkor or marasmus, it is likely that they will suffer brain impairment for the rest of their lives, even if the disease is corrected.

The first day it rained just a few sprinkles, but everyone's spirits were lifted. Then it kept raining every day with predictable downbursts. We would usually hear the rain hit our tin roof early in the morning, but by seven a.m. the sun would be shining. Then sometime in the afternoon it would cloud over again and rain. Within a week, the dried up grass turned green and the road in front of the clinic grew muddy with deep ruts. It rained almost everyday for about three weeks but after that, only a couple of times each week. Some of the dirt roads became impassible, flooded by overflow from the Juba. Mosquitoes were more plentiful, signaling the worse time of year for malaria.

Yet everyone was happy because at last there was rain. In the desert, nothing had been green for ten months, but now thorn trees suddenly began leafing. Small wildflowers appeared with yellow, white, and blue blooms. Grass thrived in the shade of acacia trees and by the footpaths. On the farms, corn and sesame sprouted and eggplants and tomatoes emerged. Life, always hard for most Somalis, now eased its burden a bit.

CHAPTER THIRTY-SEVEN

The character of a man was formed before the arguments.
—Somali Proverb

Hussein's family was now scattered between Kismayu and Mogadishu, so in early April I sent word by friends of his family in Jamama that I would like to meet with the children at the mission compound in Mogadishu. Since the trial, I had received one note from the oldest son, Omar Hussein Sadad, but Hassen Nur had struggled with translating Omar's Arabic into English. The note did indicate that he was in Mogadishu and that I needed to appeal the ruling. He signed it, "Your Friend, Omar."

Since it was now the spring rainy season, the road to Kismayu Airport was muddy but passable. The landing strip was pooled with water, but the ground was so hard it would be safe for take off. I had an hour and a half to think about my meeting with Hussein's family.

I anticipated that the gathering would be amiable, as I had always shared a good relationship with the children and their father during the hospitalization. But feelings could have changed or other extended family members might now have become involved. The Mission Board and I had agreed that we would honor the sentencing. This meant giving the family the value of one hundred camels, about 50,000 Somali shillings or five hundred shillings per camel. The total amount would translate to about $7,000 U.S. dollars. But it was possible that the family would demand more than that amount per camel.

Seven thousand dollars does not seem a great sum of money by our standards, but in 1972 the average Somali family would earn only ninety shillings, or thirteen dollars, a year. Even so, 50,000 shillings for such a large number of children would not last many years unless managed wisely. Maybe the family would not want the money in one installment for fear of its being stolen. Hassen Nur did not accompany me, and Harold was out of the country, but I was told that someone from the compound would be available to help translate.

I arrived at about two o'clock and learned that Hussein's children would arrive at four. I walked to the classroom building at the top of the hill and picked out a rather large room with a single window. There would be plenty of room no matter how many came. I had come to realize over the past year that an intended meeting with one person or one family could easily grow to a group the size of a small village. There were either eight or nine children, and I did not know how many might come. I was still at the top of the hill at four o'clock when I recognized the four young men and one young woman ascending the slope to be Hussein's children.

As they approached, I first greeted Omar, the oldest son, whom I knew the best, with a hearty hug, as friends do who have not seen each other for some time. I had not really talked to him since his father died in November, except for a short conversation the day of the trial. I greeted the other four children with a handshake. They were smiling and appeared happy to see me. I invited them into the classroom, and we sat around the largest table. They seemed to all understand most of my English, but only Omar spoke with me, and I could see that he wanted to do it in English. I felt he wanted to communicate in a direct, personal way that would be hampered if he had to rely on an interpreter.

Over the past eight months, I had learned enough Somali to help me communicate in a basic manner with patients. I could ask them where their pain was located, how long they had experienced it, what had caused it, and how they felt. I could not always understand their answers unless they were very simple. I was at a loss, though, to carry on a conversation with Omar in his native tongue. Six months of intensive language study before arriving would have helped.

Those at the table now were the oldest of Hussein's children. The girl, who was probably about fifteen years old, was shy and quiet, but I recognized her because she had stayed by her father's side and had prepared his meals during the three and a half months he was hospitalized. She was dressed in typical Somali style, with a long wrap-around and a *garbasar* over her head. They were bright in pattern, and her whole face was visible. The young men were also well groomed and wore Western-style pants and shirts. I could imagine how proud Hussein would have been of his family.

Omar served as spokesman for the group. He was the oldest, and it appeared that the rest looked up to him. At the hospital he had been the family member in charge, and he was the one his father would send to attend to important matters. Omar would occasionally turn to Ali, the Somali interpreter with us, for the translation of a word or thought to English.

After our greeting and some cordial conversation concerning my admiration for their father, I mentioned that I wanted to settle the amount of the compensation I owed them according to the judge's sentence. "I want to honor the verdict and abide by the decision of the judge," I told them. "We are not going to appeal the verdict. So we need to see how best we can take care of you."

Omar, as I expected, remained the spokesman for the group. He spoke his English so skillfully I could tell he had carefully rehearsed what he was telling me. "You were our father's friend," he said. "You took the best care of him at the hospital. We cannot take your money or the Mission's money. You must appeal the verdict." The other four siblings all nodded in agreement.

I again attempted to convey to them that this was the judge's ruling and that I accepted it and wanted to honor his decision. I appreciated their sentiments and knew we were friends, but even after they accepted the compensation, we would still be friends.

Omar then became very serious and wanted to impress upon me the significance of the situation. "We cannot take money from you. You took care of our father when he was brought to your hospital. He did not die because of your care. You gave your blood for our father. You were the only one who gave his blood for our father. You must appeal the case. You must appeal the case because the driver is the one responsible for the accident and for our father's death. You must appeal. We will not accept your money."

I was deeply touched. I had not imagined that I would not be able to talk them into accepting the blood money. I had thought that all Somalis viewed Americans as wealthy and that if they could gain some of it, the Americans would never miss it. And, in many ways, they would be correct. By their standards, we in the States have much more money than is necessary.

I loved this family. They had principles that they were going to live by, and I wondered if many people in my own culture would turn down so much money for a principle. I realized that a sense of loyalty was important to them and that through my giving of myself, especially by my donation of blood, a strong tie was forged between us.

I understood at that point that it was useless to implore Hussein's children to accept the money. I would hurt their feelings if I continued to push my decision on them. I would have to find some other way to meet the demands of the sentencing. Maybe they were right—I needed to appeal the verdict.

CHAPTER THIRTY-EIGHT

The right decision does not come by itself.
—Somali Proverb

I told the mission headquarters and my lawyer that because of the family's refusal to take the blood money, I could not fulfill the demands of the sentencing. Mennonites, throughout history, have attempted to stay out of court. They believe in living life with honesty, letting their "yes" be "yes" and their "no" mean "no," and in going the second mile and more. They believe in following the teachings of the Sermon on the Mount, no matter how difficult. The Mission Board had decided not to file an appeal, and I had agreed with their decision, although I would have preferred for my name to be cleared. Now it appeared with these new circumstances there was little left to do but appeal.

After the trial, Ibraham, my lawyer, had suggested that we not appeal the verdict because the sentencing was so light. The judge told him that the verdict would never leave the country since it would never appear on any U.S. record and would not even be attached to my passport. Ibraham was now suggesting, however, that we appeal the decision since the family would not accept the terms. The Mission Board also concurred that I should go ahead and appeal to the regional court.

After my lawyer filed an appeal brief with the court in Mogadishu, it wasn't long until I received a telegram stating that my appeal was recognized and I would be going back to court in Kismayu on the following Thursday. I was surprised and pleased by how quickly the legal system seemed to be working. I had never been involved in a court case in the States except as a witness for the defense in medical disability cases. Those cases could be strung out for months or even years and appeal cases lasted even longer.

Since it was the middle of April and we were now well into the rainy season, the road from Jamama to the tarmac was impassable even with the four-wheel drive Land Rover. Truck drivers said, however, that we could make it to Kismayu if we took a route that ran north for fifteen miles before it turned south.

Hassen Nur and I left early on that Thursday morning, prepared for any road hazard. Mary had packed us a lunch, and we brought along ropes, boots, and sandbags in case we got stuck. We knew it was important in the rainy season to get started in the right tire ruts, and, if we became mired, we hoped a large lorry would come along to pull us free.

But as it turned out, we had no problems on the road and arrived in plenty of time. In fact, we had to wait for the regularly scheduled flight from Mogadishu to arrive with the appeals court judge, my lawyer, and other members of the court.

This appeal involved only my part of the trial. Again, there were five languages used: Somali for conversation, Italian for the legal language, Arabic for the recorder and his typewriter, Russian for the autopsy report, and English for me when my lawyer felt I needed to know what had just been said. The judge asked me to verify that I really was a doctor. I always carried that documentation with me for any official business. I showed him my diploma from medical school, my Indiana medical license, a letter from Paul Bender the administrator of Wells Community Hospital, and a letter from the Somali Ministry of Health. These papers seemed to satisfy him.

The judge asked a few additional questions about Hussein's hospitalized condition, but mostly he conversed with my lawyer. Hassen Nur informed me afterward that most of the discussion centered on how to word the decision following the hearing.

The case was over in two hours, and the officials hurried to the airport to catch the return flight which had been waiting for them. Before he left the court building, my attorney told me he thought everything went well and that I would probably hear from the judge within a week.

CHAPTER THIRTY-NINE

Justice knows only Allah.
—Somali Proverb

Two weeks later, as I was seeing patients after my tea break, Hassen Nur stepped into my examination room with a telegram. Although there was no telephone service in the southern part of Somali, there was telegraphic service between Jamama and Mogadishu. I was anxious to open the telegram, and, after excusing myself, I walked out to the courtyard with Hassen Nur. The telegram, which was in Italian, was short but meaningful. Hassen Nur said it was from the judge in Mogadishu and stated that I was exonerated of all charges that had been brought against me. Suddenly, I felt what a Somali woman must feel at the end of a long trek when a load of sticks or a rack of rocks is taken off her head.

I told Hassen Nur that he could inform the nurses, and I immediately hurried to our house to share the good news with Mary. She and Hawa were preparing lunch as I rushed in, saying, "The judge found me innocent! I'm free!" We thought we had reached the point where we could accept any verdict, but this was a great relief. Soon all the mission and hospital personnel knew the outcome as well. Finally, we all felt vindicated and relieved. Our prayers that evening were ones of thanks.

Over the years I have used the left-handed bowline knot to tie a boat to a dock or our horse to a tree. It's a good knot for security since it's hard to loosen. Soon after receiving my telegram, I began to understand that I had been caught in a kind of left-handed bowline knot. Hassen Nur found out that the initial judge in Kismayu and the prosecuting attorney were close friends of the driver involved in the accident. They had felt that if they could convict the doctor for Hussein's death, then the driver would not be responsible for paying blood money. They felt that the mission hospital could easily afford the payment, and, since I would be kept out of jail, I would readily agree to the terms.

They had not counted on Hussein's family refusing to accept payment from me and the mission. In fact, it was not until the family initially went to court to collect the blood money from the driver that my involvement was even mentioned. When the judge questioned the driver, he responded that he couldn't be guilty because the doctor at the hospital let Hussein die.

I knew that the lawyer for the driver was also Dr. Urquhart's lawyer, but I did not know until after the acquittal that my lawyer was also the lawyer for the insurance company. This may explain why in court very few questions were asked of the driver and why my lawyer had so little to say.

I also learned that at some point after my first trial, Ibraham, my lawyer, had heard from President Barre who said to him, "You need to appeal the case against the American to the regional court. He will be found innocent." I will never know why Barre interceded on my behalf. Was it because of internal pressure from within Somalia? Could it have been political pressure from the United States Ambassador, E. Ross Adair, in neighboring Ethiopia? Or did President Barre hear a still, small voice speak to him?

At first I heard that Hussein's family was going to appeal their case to the supreme court of the country for reparation from the driver and his insurance company. However, before we left Somalia, the government, as Hussein's former employer, paid full compensation to his family.

I admired Hussein's children, not only for their support of their father during his long hospitalization but also for their strong beliefs about right and wrong even amid a multitude of pressures. They could not be swayed by lawyers, judges, or the lure of easy money. These were truly exceptional people.

I was finally cleared of all guilt. The appeals court judge confirmed that "no criminal conduct was traced from the obtained proof such as witnesses, autopsy, hospital register, and the patient's clinic card." He added that the death was due to natural causes that occurred after the operation and "thus the SHOCK was not caused by any negligence and imprudence of Dr. Miller." He concluded with "we do not hide that being convinced of the innocence of the accused, the taking place of the confuted judgment was a matter of great surprise."

This verdict was an answer to the many prayers that had been offered on my behalf. Although the experience had been a difficult one, it had brought all the mission workers and Somali believers closer together and had demonstrated to us the need for support and fellowship from all of our spiritual family. It had also brought me closer to the Jamama community. Now I was no longer the mission doctor; I was *their* doctor.

We do not know the ways of God, but we do know God is faithful and will not put us through more than we can bear. Being accused and found guilty of murder was not the straw that broke the camel's back. God gives us the strength and patience to tolerate what is before us. Somali nomads travel along century-old migratory paths in the desert. They don't know if there will be water and pasture for their cattle, camels, and families when they arrive at the next camp site. They rely on some past experience but travel mostly by faith that Allah will provide. As the Somali proverb says, "Allah himself helps a simple man to find a good place for his camp."

The nomad wonders, "Will there be rain this season? Will the well water be clear? Will I be welcomed by friends when I arrive?" The nomad learns patience as he travels those dusty trails. And I had to learn that same kind of patience, a "waiting on the Lord" kind of fortitude that has helped me in later decades when I have faced trials.

The six weeks between my exoneration and our departure from Somalia were pleasant ones. Our daughters had returned from school and were enjoying playing with friends and all of our pet animals. Shari and Marlis particularly liked the Kurtz's monkey, Jack. He was so tame that he'd perch on shoulders and heads. The girls occasionally came to the hospital and spent time with the nurses and teachers. Stephen was happier with his sisters around to read to him during the day, and Abdi was getting more expressive, delighting in all the attention he received. During this time, Mary was pleased that her whole family was home, but she was increasingly busy with cooking, washing, and sewing, and, of course, making arrangements for the trip back to the States.

Many Somalis stopped in to visit before we left, and sometimes they asked if there was anything we weren't taking home. If so, they would be happy to accept it. We told them that the household items had been left by the previous doctors and that we would be leaving them for the next doctor and his family. A number of women wanted to buy Mary's black wig. I had worn its long, straight tresses at a Halloween party we held for all the compound personnel. Since then, several community women had come to our house to borrow the wig when they wanted their picture taken. Mary solved this dilemma by giving the wig to a young man, the town barber, who was also the town photographer since he owned a camera. That way, everyone was happy. Anyone could have her picture taken with the wig.

With our year of medical mission coming to an end, the accident which occurred the day before we arrived was now finally behind us.

CHAPTER FORTY

You will not remain—let a good memory of you remain.
—Somali Proverb

As the airplane lifted off, I took my last look at Mogadishu. I could see the flat roofs of houses and shops and then, rising above them, the delicate minarets of four white mosques. Higher, I saw the rounded huts on the city's outskirts and the ocean where waves crawled forward toward the same beach where we spread our blankets that first Sunday and waded into the warmth.

As we flew south, I followed the sand dunes and a landscape that was still slightly green from the spring rainy season. Over the last year I had made the trip between Mogadishu and Kismayu six times on Somali Airlines and twice overland, but now I was headed to Nairobi on East African Airways. This would be my last view of Somalia. Flying over Kismayu, I felt a surge of grief wash over me as I took my last look at the Indian Ocean and thought of the friends I was leaving behind. For as long as I could, I watched the brown Juba snaking its way through a long *garbasar* of green and then looked down at the parched desert, the small villages, the low, flat acacias.

We kept ascending until the ground was far below. Finally, I sat back and thought about my recent send-off from Jamama.

Mary and the children had departed one week earlier to meet Mary's sister, Marty, in Nairobi. She had spent the past year teaching at an elementary school in Liberia and was now flying back with us through Europe to the States. The farewell parties for us had taken place before my family left, and this last week had been a busy one for me. I taught some classes at the nursing school for the returning second year students and saw dozens of patients who wished to visit a last time before I left or who were scheduled for a follow-up. Since Ron Lowen, the doctor replacing me, would arrive the next week, I only performed emergency surgeries, but I made hospital rounds twice each day.

Saying good-bye to Hassen Nur was extremely emotional. He and I had worked side-by-side during the year. We had often traveled together, and I had depended on him for Somali language and cultural interpretation. We had prayed together in difficult situations, and he had accompanied and supported me throughout the court case.

I also said good-bye to each of the Somali nurses and students and to the hospital maintenance personnel. I couldn't contain my tears as I realized I would probably never see them again. I felt anxiety about what lay ahead for them in the future. They each had a vision for self-improvement and service to their community. Already, they had achieved so much, but what would happen to them if the schools and hospital were closed or nationalized, as it appeared they might be? There were always rumors that this would come to pass. The few industries were now nationalized, and, in March, the importation of medicine was placed under government control.

Saying good-bye to Martha and Pauline was hard also, but we said we would see each other again in the States. The Kurtzes had left two weeks earlier and had been replaced by the Brubaker family.

On the Sunday before leaving, I met with the Swahili-speaking Bantu believers from along the river for a church service and a farewell. Over the years, they were accustomed to seeing mission workers come and go. I recalled the foot-washing and communion services we had held during the past year. Washing the feet of these brothers and sisters had seemed an appropriate symbol of humility and service since, to reach us, they had walked in sandals five miles on dusty paths.

I had gone to baby Abdi's house to visit him before I left and saw that he was still happy and cooing. His aunts received me warmly, and I could see that he was bonding with them. During the year, I had had the feeling at times that his father wanted us to adopt Abdi, but I could sense that the women in his family would oppose it. I hoped Abdi would grow to be a leader in his community, possibly even a doctor.

Before landing in Nairobi, my thoughts shot forward, and I wondered how I would make the transition back into the medical practice and how my new experiences would affect my outlook. What changes would have occurred in the medical field? I did know that if I saw patients with tuberculosis, malaria, or hookworm, I would be ready for them.

EPILOGUE

A day organized by the call of the muezzin to prayer became a day arranged by a lengthy list of activities. Soon I was back working twelve hour days, plus taking my share of night call and weekends. Our children busied themselves with school and church activities—Cub scouts and swim team for Stephen, piano and 4-H for Marlis and Shari. Mary stayed busy transporting the children to meetings and helping with music and children's programs at church. Eventually, she kept accounting books for the Markle Hardware Store and, later, became co-founder and editor of *The Markle Times*, a monthly newspaper.

Soon after our return, I started an Emergency Medical Technician (EMT) training program at Wells Community Hospital and worked to coordinate services for northern Indiana. I served on the Northern Wells Community School Board for eight years, participated in Lions Club, and was appointed to the board of directors of our local bank.

Frequently, I would remember fondly that year in Somali without all of the extra activities. In many ways, life was simpler then. I could walk a few hundred feet to the clinic and come home for lunch and a couple hours of rest. I could work at my own pace and patients didn't get upset about waiting. There were no appointment schedules, and, other than an old-fashioned ringer-type telephone we used within the mission compound, there were no telephone interruptions and no telemarketing. We had always spent time with our children, but a year without television gave us more time together to read and play games. I had also shared more time with Mary, watching the sunset and stars.

Somali tea had been different from any drink I ever tasted. Every mid-morning and afternoon, I had looked forward to my tea break. Mary and I tried brewing Somali tea when we returned home but never achieved anything close to the flavor. Getting the mail has never been the same in the States, either. We don't talk about the mail or even look forward to its coming. It mainly consists of bills and ads, anyway. The life-saving rain we anxiously anticipated for months has become something we take for granted.

During the first several years back, Mary and I presented talks and slide shows to many civic and church groups. These programs helped us feel connected to Somalia and the people we knew there. But over time these presentations dwindled. Instead, every two or three years, we would pull out our slides to show to the family. We would wonder about Hassen Nur and Omar and Hawa. Were they still in Jamama? Were they safe? Were they refugees in northern Kenya where Mennonites were providing aid?

We always calculated Abdi's age and wondered what he might be doing. When Martha and Pauline left Jamama, they told us that at fourteen months Abdi was not looking very healthy. They had last seen him at the hospital when they treated him for malaria. Before Elsie left Jamama, though, she sent us a photo of Abdi at age two, perched on the hood of a vehicle and apparently healthy. Abdi would be thirty-eight years old now if he survived childhood diseases and all of the political turmoil.

The Markle doctors continued to feel concern for those who need medical care in developing countries. After we returned from Somalia, Lee Kinzer spent two months in the

Congo and then Vic Binkley, our surgeon, served a year in Bangladesh with his family. In 1976 the Church of God, head-quartered in Findley, Ohio, asked if the Markle doctors would help establish a medical mission in Haiti to go along with their schools, churches and nutritional centers. We helped develop the new clinic's programs, design its buildings, and hire its personnel. We numbered five doctors in our medical group by then, and we all felt that, because of our families, we could commit to only short mission trips.

During the 1980s we enlarged the clinic in Haiti and added a maternity ward for deliveries. In the mid-1990s we opened a hospital for surgeries and to care for most illnesses. Now, four Haitian doctors work full time at the clinic and hospital, and the director of the hospital is a doctor who grew up in Pierre Payen.

For the last two decades with world news often centering on Middle East conflict and terrorism, I have felt more in tune with these current events because of my year in Somalia. Due to Somalia's location on the Horn of Africa, across the Gulf of Aden from Yemen and Saudi Arabia, it almost seems, geographically, to be part of the Middle East. Its Islamic identity also ties it strongly to the Arab states. And, yet, because Somalia is in Africa, my concern for that country also connects me to the clan warfare, genocide, famines, and poverty in places such as Sudan, Upper Volta, Rwanda, and Central African Republic. In these countries, as in Somalia, the need for humanitarian aid is great.

Sometimes when I'm disheartened by the violence in the world and fear that the gulf of misunderstanding between Christians and Muslims is only growing wider and deeper, I remember that for over fifty years Mennonites and Somalis have been crossing that gulf, forming friendships and working together, despite cultural differences and fears.

In particular, I think back to one April afternoon in Mogadishu when Hussein's children walked up the steep hill to meet me. I remember how Omar wouldn't take the blood money, the price of a hundred camels, that I was prepared to pay. What was on his mind was not the blood of retribution, but the blood I had shared with his father—how that made us kinsmen, true blood brothers in the human clan.

SOMALIA SINCE 1972

Nearly forty years have passed since our family left Somalia. For most of those years, until recently, I would rarely see a news story from the Horn of Africa. Only periodic military clashes have been of sufficient importance to fill a small box on the inside page of the newspaper under "Other World News."

At the time we left, at the end of July 1972, the mission board operated a hospital, nursing school, and an intermediate school in Jamama. It also opened a new secondary school with dormitories for two hundred students in Jowhar and an intermediate school, an agricultural project, a maternity ward and a medical clinic at Mahaday. In Mogadishu and Kismayu, adult evening classes in business and English were offered and, in downtown Mogadishu, a mission bookshop, New Africa Booksellers, sold English readers and other educational books.

In October 1972, only three months after we had left Somalia, the government nationalized all the mission's schools and medical facilities. Dr. Loewen and his family left Somalia at that time, but the nurses remained for several more months. In December that year, all the properties, facilities, and equipment were nationalized without compensation. Several teachers stayed on and taught in government high schools and in the university, living in rented apartments, until all personnel connected with the mission were asked to leave in April 1976.

In 1975 and '76 severe drought and famine scourged the land. Some relief aid reached the people, but thousands of Somalis died. General Siad Barre was still in power and viewed as a ruthless dictator by an increasing number of Somalis.

When Somalia invaded the Ogaden in 1977, Russian forces were expelled from Somalia for their support of Ethiopia. Development programs by then were few, and educational efforts seemed to be deteriorating. The government endorsed the use of Latin script for the writing of the Somali language in October 1972, but only a small percentage of children attended school, and even fewer were learning to read and write Somali. Over the years, skirmishes with neighboring Ethiopia seemed the only glue that kept people united and President Barre's government in control.

In the 1980s, the government did invite some Mennonite mission workers to enter the country again to help with agricultural and nutritional programs as well as other community development projects in Mogadishu, Merka, and Kismayu. However, in 1989, all Mennonite Central Committee volunteers left the country due to rising inter- and sub-clan violence. By 1990, all Eastern Mennonite Mission personnel had left.

Armed opposition to Barre began in northern Somalia in 1988. In early 1991, clan-based militias removed Barre from power, and the ousted leader fled to Nigeria where, four years later, he died in exile. A headline in January 1991 read, "President Mohamed Siad Barre Is Overthrown by Clan-based Rebels, Who Quickly Turn on One Another."

Massive UN relief operations began in April 1992, but more than 100,000 people died of hunger and clan-related violence between 1991 and 1992. Americans remember Somali militiamen shooting down the U.S. Black Hawk helicopter in Mogadishu and the eighteen U.S. servicemen who died in the crash and in the subsequent rescue attempt. The main images many U.S. citizens have of Somalia are violent ones from the 2001 movie, *Black Hawk Down.*

In March 1994, U.S. troops withdrew from Somalia, leaving a United Nation's Peacekeeping Operation in place. Then, in 1995, Marines escorted the last peacekeepers from the country.

In summer 2006, militias loyal to the Islamic Courts Union drove the warlords from Mogadishu and then pushed southward over the next several months to gain control of cities and villages, all the way to the Kenyan border. A UN-backed parliament met for the first time inside Somalia in February that year, but this governmental body controlled only Baidoa and a small area around that city.

In January 2007, headlines read, "Jets Bomb Somali Airports; Ethiopian Troops Capture Town." The UN-backed government, with the aid of the Ethiopian military, was taking control of the nation by driving those loyal to the Islamic Courts Union out of the country or underground to fight in skirmishes and bombings. The invasion by Ethiopian forces had the approval of the United States, which accused the Islamic Union of Courts of sheltering al Qaeda operatives.

Conflict and fighting have plagued Somalia for centuries, but now attacks involve grenade launchers, jet bombers, and automatic machine guns. According to an Amnesty International Report in May, 2008, "Soldiers, insurgents and bandits routinely target civilians in Somalia for rape, robbery and murder." Gang rape is common, and so is a type of killing called "slaughtering" or "killing like goats" in which the victim's throat is slit, frequently in front of loved ones. In the past two years, more than 16,000 civilians have died as a result of the conflict and one million people have become refugees. The UN has cited the ten-mile camp along a road outside of Mogadishu as probably the largest concentration of displaced people in the world, with a population of 250,000 in April 2008.

As discouraged Ethiopian troops started pulling out of Somalia during the last weeks of that year, Former President Abdulla Yusuf Ahmed, who opposed expanding parliament to include the opposition, resigned under international pressure. In an election held in January 2009 in Djibouti, legislators chose moderate Islamist leader Sheikh Sharif Ahmed as the new Somali president. According to David Clarke of the BBC, "Analysts say that Ahmed has a real chance of reuniting Somalis, given his Islamist roots and acceptability to other sides. But reconciling Somalia's ten million people and stopping eighteen years of bloodshed in the Horn of Africa nation remain a daunting task even for him." Hard-line Islamic insurgents called al Shabaab ("Lads" in Somali) have declared the election meaningless and say they will continue fighting.

Will the factions ever unite so that the greeting, *Nabad waya*, "Yes, it is peace," can take on its full meaning? In 1971-1972, we met many Somalis who wanted education, freedom from disease and poverty, and the opportunity to live peacefully with their neighbors. Many, I am sure, still desire these things and even more fervently.

Mennonites are one group that has not abandoned the Somalis over the past fifty years. After the fall of Barre's government in 1991, Eastern Mennonite Mission (EMM) and Mennonite Central Committee (MCC) together established an office in Nairobi from which they continued to interact with Somalis. For much of the 1990s, this office supported grassroot activities carried out by Somalis keen on peace building, education initiatives and advocacy for refugees.

More recently, Mennonites have worked with and helped fund Somali Non-Government Organizations (NGOs) that carry out a spectrum of services. NGOs provide aid to internally displaced Somalis, operate community-based schools, hold peace training workshops in secondary schools, develop microcredit-education programs, and work to raise awareness of health problems associated with HIV/Aids and female circumcision. Through these humanitarian programs, displacement camps have obtained collapsible water bladders and illiterate Somali women have received what they need to start their own businesses—literacy and business training and micro-finance loans. NGOs have provided children with scholarships to attend community-based schools; they have taught secondary school students and teachers how to mediate conflicts in their schools, families, and neighborhoods.

As members of a denomination with a strong belief in non-violence, Mennonites in 2007-2008 contributed to Somali Peace Line, an organization that promotes mediation skills through workshops in Mogadishu's secondary schools. More than eight hundred students and forty-seven teachers in twenty-nine schools have received these peace training classes. According to Ann King-Grosh, former country representative to Somalia for MCC and EMM, the students, in addition to mediating conflicts in the school and at home, "have gotten involved with calling for a short cease fire so that classmates could safely leave a school in a conflict area." In another new peace venture, Eastern Mennonite University, through its Center for Justice and Peacebuilding, is helping a university in Somaliland set up a conflict resolution curriculum.

Some of the Mennonites who have returned to Somalia to participate in peace conferences or other humanitarian efforts are themselves from a Somali background. In 1992, Ahmed Haile lost his lower leg to an anti-aircraft shell at a peace gathering in Mogadishu. Two years later, he journeyed to Nairobi to teach peace studies and reconciliation at a university. Ahmed currently instructs students from such war-torn countries as Rwanda, Congo, Burundi, and Southern Sudan.

In recent correspondence with Asli Aden Ashkir, one of my nursing students who arrived in the States ten years ago, I learned some information about a few of the Somali nurses and staff with whom I worked. Lul Abdi, the receptionist whose wedding feast Mary attended, now lives in the United States, as does Lul's sister, Dahabo Abdi, and her husband, Mohamud Balo, both of whom were students in my nursing class. Ali Omar Yussuf, one of the nurses, became a doctor and worked in

Saudi Arabia until his death from natural causes. Ugo, one of the male nurses, resides in the States, while Abdi Gure lives in Mogadishu. Unfortunately, Abdi's wife, Mariam Mohamed Hassen, another of my nursing students, died in a shooting four years ago.

In 2005 Asli met Omar, the young man who helped Mary with housework in the evenings. They were both attending a nursing education meeting in Bahrain. Omar had received his nursing degree in India and then worked in Saudi Arabia for a long period of time before returning to Somalia. He told Asli that he had been asked to lead the new nursing program at Somali University and that his son was studying medicine in Mogadishu. We asked Asli if she knew the whereabouts of Hassen Nur or Abdi Hakim, but she didn't know. She said that when she last visited Jamama, in 1985, about half of the hospital was being used for health care and the other half housed donkeys and other livestock.

Somalia is still an extremely poor country. Only 1.67 percent of the land is arable, and the median age is not much over seventeen. Soaring food prices, caused by the devaluation of Somali shillings and a prolonged drought, have caused riots in Mogadishu, where it is particularly hard for the urban poor to obtain food.

Unfortunately, piracy and violence against humanitarian workers threaten the availability of food aid. The United Nations has announced it will cut off food distribution unless attacks against workers cease. In the early months of 2008, the UN's refugee agency deemed the situation in Somalia the "world's most pressing humanitarian crisis." A spokesperson also described it as "a forgotten crisis."

But, like a thorn tree blossoming in the desert, a sign of hope appeared on March 25, 2008, when the UN World Health Organization announced that polio has been eradicated in Somalia. WHO called it a "landmark victory" and a testimony to the dedicated work of 10,000 volunteers who, despite the violence in the country, vaccinated more than 1.8 million children under age five and entered every household multiple times. Ali Mao Moallim was one of these volunteers. He was the last person on earth to catch smallpox more than three decades ago. "Somalia was the last country with smallpox," he said. "I wanted to help ensure that we would not be the last place with polio, too."

Somalia is a country in dire need of the kind of teamwork that brought together those ten thousand volunteer workers. It needs the kind of compassionate, forward-looking leadership and cooperation that has brought Mennonites and Somalis together for the past fifty years. In general, a willingness to work together and a mutual respect for cultural differences and religious views have characterized this relationship.

"If you come to the one-eyed people's country, pull out your eye," advises one Somali proverb that seems to endorse an attitude of empathy when visiting another culture. My father, Perry J. Miller, paraphrased Ezekiel 3:15 to create his own proverb endorsing empathy: "I sat where they sat and was amazed for seven days." He used this passage to emphasize the necessity of trying to walk in another's shoes or sandals, of seeing from another's perspective. When we do that, we start to experience that message so central to both the Bible and the Qur'an: We are all God's children.

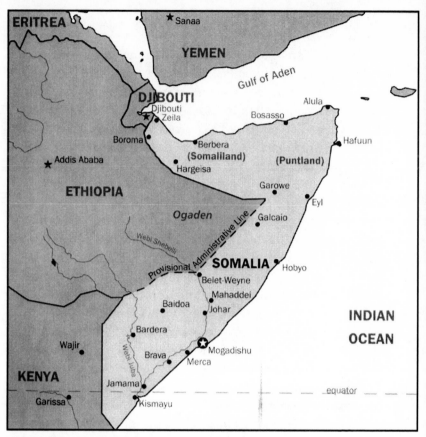

Spellings vary for place names in Somalia.

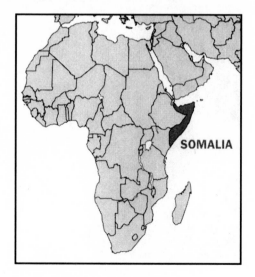

Maps taken from Omar Eby, *Fifty Years, Fifty Stories: The Mennonite Mission in Somalia, 1953-2003* (DreamSeeker Books, 2003). Used by permission of Cascadia Publishing House, all rights reserved.

ABOUT THE AUTHOR

Gerald L. Miller, M.D., was born in Goshen, Indiana, and grew up in nearby Shipshewana, in a Mennonite family with a strong lineage of teachers and missionaries. As a child, Gerald enjoyed listening to relatives like Orie O. Miller and Jay Hostetler recount their international experiences at the dinner table or on Sundays at Forks Mennonite Church.

As a student at Goshen College, Gerald studied premed and, after graduating from Indiana School of Medicine, set up a family practice in the small town of Markle, Indiana. For forty-two years, he worked in this largely rural area south of Ft. Wayne. During this time Gerald regularly made house calls to those unable to come to the office and developed community home health care and Hospice services. To provide better emergency care for his patients, he helped his community develop the first EMT and Paramedic services in northeast Indiana.

This book tells the story of Gerald's year of service with Eastern Mennonite Mission Board in Somalia, East Africa, but over the last thirty-two years, he has also made twenty-five trips to Project Help in Haiti. There, with the effort of other doctors in his medical practice and support from the Church of God, he helped establish a medical clinic and then a hospital.

Since 2006, Gerald and his wife Mary have been living in Westfield, Indiana, where he enjoys gardening, golfing, playing card games with his grandchildren, and indulging an eclectic taste in literature, from nineteenth-century Russian novels to John Grisham mysteries. He and Mary enjoy traveling and recently toured Paraguay with a group of friends from their church, First Mennonite of Indianapolis.

ABOUT THE EDITOR

Shari Wagner started writing poems the year she was in Somalia. As an eighth grader, she started pecking out metaphors about the desert on the same manual typewriter her mother used to give typing lessons to her Somali students. Shari wanted to capture the harsh and desolate beauty of a landscape that stood in contrast to the maple-lined streets of Goshen, Indiana, where she was born, and to the cornfields that surrounded her wooded home near Markle. She didn't know it then, but Somalia is a land of poets where proverbs are used extensively and personal honor hinges on an ability to compose and recite poems.

Evening Chore, Shari's first book of poems was published in 2005 by DreamSeeker Books (imprint of Cascadia Publishing House), and her poems have appeared in numerous magazines, including *The Christian Century, Christianity & Literature, North American Review, Southern Poetry Review,* and *Black Warrior Review.* An upcoming issue of *Shenandoah* will include her essay, "Camels, Cowries & a Poem for Aisha," written in memory of Aisha Ibrahim Duhulow, a thirteen-year-old Somali girl stoned to death last year in Kismayu. Over the years, she has received six grants from the Indiana Arts Commission and two fellowships from the Arts Council of Indianapolis. She holds a B.A. in English and Communication from Goshen College and an M.F.A. in Creative Writing from Indiana University.

Shari teaches poetry writing for the Writers' Center of Indiana and lives in Westfield, Indiana, with her husband Chuck, a poet and English teacher, and daughters Vienna and Iona. The whole family enjoys excursions to Indiana's state parks.

ABOUT THE ARTIST

Vienna Wagner is a sophomore at Brebeuf Jesuit Preparatory School in Indianapolis and hopes to have a career that combines her interests in art, writing, and environmental science. She currently works as a volunteer with Art with a Heart, an after-school enrichment program for elementary students, and she also enjoys playing softball, acting in theater, and attending movies with friends. Vienna's favorite 4-H project has been working with a member of the Camelidae family—a llama that helped her win Grand Champion in Showmanship at the county fair.

In creating her Sufi-inspired, camel mandala (see cover), Vienna incorporated various details related to Somalia and to this book: minarets, acacia trees, the Somali flag, an Islamic design, and the Arabic translation of "A Hundred Camels." She learned how to draw mandalas from her high school art teacher, Joe Cancilla.

CPSIA information can be obtained
at www.ICGtesting.com
Printed in the USA
FFOW03n1944091115
18450FF